Workers' Rights, East and West

A comparative study of trade union and workers' rights in Western democracies and Eastern Europe

Adrian Karatnycky
Alexander J. Motyl
Adolph Sturmthal

League for Industrial Democracy

Transaction Books
New Brunswick (U.S.A.) and London (U.K.)

Workers' Rights, East and West

ISBN 0-87855-867-5

Table of Contents

Preface

This study examines the status of worker and trade union rights in a select group of Western industrial democracies, and a similar group of countries in the Soviet bloc. The study's purpose is to elevate the issue of worker rights to a more prominent place in the broad human rights debate. Each of the countries discussed here has signed the Helsinki Accords, and is bound by that charter's human rights provisions. While the Helsinki agreement does not specifically deal with the question of workers' rights, a number of its provisions are clearly applicable to the rights of working people. Each of these countries has also signed relevant International Labor Organization conventions, which carry the force of international law.

The countries examined are also similar in that all have large concentrations of heavy industry. These are clearly developed countries with large, industrial work forces and substantial labor movements.

The authors assessed the degree of trade union and worker rights in each country with four criteria in mind: the right of workers to band together, organize collectively, and engage in bargaining with private enterprise or the state; the right to strike; the degree of internal union democracy; and the ability of the various labor movements to pursue political objectives on behalf of the working classes. The right to trade union organization and collective bargaining is recognized both by the Universal Declaration of Human Rights and the International Labor Organization. The other criteria, as well, are essential to the ability of a trade union to protect the interests of its members, and expand the democratic liberties of working people. The absence of these rights ensures that trade unions will either be powerless to achieve the full range of rights and liberties for its members, or, more likely, that the labor movement will be made subservient to the goals of an all-powerful state or political party, or the whims of the employer.

In assessing each of the labor movements examined here, an effort was made to evaluate both the laws relating to workers and trade unions, as well as the state of worker rights as they exist in reality. This is especially important in dealing with Communist governments. Each of the four Communist countries has adopted laws extending broad powers to trade unions. In reality, however, trade unions in these countries are controlled by the state and independent action by unions is not permitted (until, that is, the events in Poland during 1980). On the other hand, the Communist regimes have enacted laws and regulations which clearly restrict many worker rights which are universally accepted as essential in the democratic world.

There are, obviously, certain problems in attempting to apply similar standards to trade unions in Communist and democratic countries. It will be argued that trade unions patterned after the Communist model serve different functions and pursue different goals than do trade unions in the democracies. The standards used in this study, however, are universal in application. Moreover, Communist governments themselves repeatedly assert that their unions adhere to democratic standards; that, in fact, they are more democratic than unions in the West. These governments have also signed the Universal Declaration of Human Rights and various ILO conventions, and can thus be judged by the standards set down in those documents.

A further problem relates to source material. There is an abundance of literature on the rights of workers and unions in the West, ranging from official government studies, independent scholarly and journalistic investigations, and a great deal of other reliable material. In each of the Western countries assessed, the trade unions are subject to criticism from a variety of sources: political figures, academicians, conservatives and businessmen who believe unions wield too much power, radicals who believe unions are insufficiently militant, and discontented trade unionists themselves. In the Communist world, on the other hand, there are really only three reliable sources: the laws which govern workers and unions, dissident critics and emigre workers (the possible exception, again, being Poland), and reports issued by the ILO. Until trade unions in the Soviet bloc achieve a measure of independence from the state and a truly free flow of information is possible, those addressing the question of trade union rights in these countries must labor under the constraints imposed by their totalitarian systems.

Professor Adolph Sturmthal is the author of the section dealing with the Western democracies. Adrian Karatnycky wrote the studies of the Soviet Union and Rumania, and Alexander J. Motyl wrote the studies of Poland and Czechoslovakia.

A.P.

Acknowledgments

The League for Industrial Democracy was fortunate in having the invaluable assistance of a number of individuals in the preparation of this study. A special debt of gratitude is owed to Professor Roy Godson, director of the International Labor Program of Georgetown University, and to Professor William Douglas, of the ILP, for their encouragement and advice. We would also like to express thanks to Daniel Horowitz for his manuscript suggestions and overall advice.

This study would not have been possible without the generosity of the Joyce Mertz-Gilmore Foundation and the Scaife Family Charitable Trusts.

We are also indebted to Charles Bloomstein and Tom Kahn, and to the Committee for the Defense of Soviet Political Prisoners, whose work provided the inspiration for this study.

Foreword

By Arch Puddington

Trade unions have emerged during the twentieth century as accepted and influential institutions in democratic industrial societies. Millions of workers belong to labor unions, and they benefit—as, to a significant extent, do non-union workers—from the social and economic policies embodied in the programs of their unions. Where free unions exist workers are protected against capricious acts of management. Their lives and the lives of their families are enriched by the fringe benefits secured through union initiatives. In many countries minimum wage rates—enacted because of the prodding of trade unions—provide a measure of equity for workers in the most poorly paid (and often non-union) industries. Unions have also played the principal role in pressing for the enactment of regulations which prohibit certain job safety hazards and which limit worker contact with disease-producing substances.

The achievements of trade unions go well beyond the workplace issues or even the material gains won for union members. As the remarkable events in Poland during the summer of 1980 dramatically illustrate, the appeal of trade unionism embraces fundamental questions of freedom and human liberty. This appeal, the appeal of bread *and* freedom, is universal. Thus, the struggle for genuine trade union rights—entailing, for example, the right to elect workers' representatives without the meddling of an all-powerful political party or state—is an integral part of the struggle for broader human rights. However assured other human rights may appear to be, in the absence of trade union and worker rights, wage earners—and here we are talking about the overwhelming majority in modern industrial society—cannot have the substance and reality of other rights. On the other hand, trade union rights cannot exist in reality in the absence of general human rights, for without such rights as freedom of assembly, of dissent, without the right to move about one's own country or across national boundaries, or the right to a free press or free speech, trade union rights cannot be exercised, even though they may be inscribed in law.

Unfortunately, the essential relationship between free trade unions and human rights is often overlooked in the democratic world. This is particularly regrettable because the development of free trade unions stands as one of the most impressive accomplishments of democratic forms of government and also because free trade unions have been among the strongest supporters of the democratic idea and general human rights. For trade unionists, democracy is more than an abstract principle. Trade unions, in fighting for the rights of workers, played central roles in building the fabric of modern democratic society. One need only make a cursory examination of trade union history in the United States to be reminded that the acceptance of trade unions was earned only after long years of struggle and sacrifice. It is a tribute to the determination and will of the labor activists of an earlier era that they overcame the hostility—sometimes violently expressed—of powerful employers and often of political authorities in the process of winning legitimacy as an accepted part of society. But is is also important to remember that without the existence of democratic institutions in these countries, no matter how imperfectly they may have functioned, the rights of working people would never have been achieved. It may be true that democratic rights do not by themselves guarantee justice for working people, but it is without question that democracy's absence renders justice for workers an impossibility.

We are constantly reminded of this fact as we observe events in countries which have fallen under Communist domination. It is one of the ironies of our age that a system which claims to speak for workers' interests inevitably denies workers their rights. In the four Communist countries assessed in this study and, indeed, in all Communist societies, we find that the very legitimacy of independent trade unions and worker rights is rejected. To be sure, Communist countries include in their constitutions and labor codes stirring declarations of how the working classes and their trade union organizations are entitled to play the "leading role" in the creation of a "socialist" system which the workers presumably own.

In reality, of course, the workers have no rights in societies where all power—political, social, and economic—is monopolized by the party and state. The Communist countries examined here all have established organizations called trade unions, but these organizations do not carry out the functions of authentic workers' organizations. Rather, the "trade unions" in the Communist world perform functions of discipline, social control, and administration as an integral part of the party and state monopoly of power. These organizations are so fundamentally different from the independent trade unions in democratic countries that the term *trade union* is really inappropriate to describe them.

If the fraudulent nature of the Communist trade union "model" was not perfectly obvious before the wave of strikes and worker protest in Poland during the summer of 1980, it should certainly be clear to all in the aftermath of that historic confrontation. The events in Poland have served to demolish a number of myths about the relationship between workers' rights in particular and the struggle for human rights in general. To begin with, it can no longer be argued with any plausibility that the only people dissatisfied with the state of human rights in the Communist world are a miniscule group of discontented intellectuals, and that the overwhelming majority of workers are satisfied with their lot. Although worker protest has not been expressed on the mass scale of Poland in other Communist countries, the evidence clearly suggests that the potential for similar outbursts exists throughout Eastern Europe. The testimony of both dissidents and ordinary workers who have emigrated to the West indicates that workers in Prague, Gorky, Bucharest, and Budapest have no more faith in the official labor organizations of their countries than the workers of Gdansk did in the government-controlled Polish unions. Given the opportunity, workers throughout Eastern Europe would raise the same demands as their Polish counterparts: a higher standard of living and trade union organizations controlled by the workers themselves.

The demands of the Polish workers' opposition for an end to censorship and for a free press are of special significance. The issue of free speech and the right to publish free of state interference is, of course, an essential right for democratic societies. But these rights have a unique and very particular relevance to trade unions. To understand the full significance of this fact, we need only recall that one of the bloodiest worker eruptions in this century—the 1962 general strike in Novocherkassk in the Soviet Union—took place unbeknown to either Soviet citizens or the outside world. For practical purposes this strike—which cost the lives of between one hundred and three hundred workers, forced the intervention of the military, and brought brutal reprisals to surviving participants—might never have occurred. At the time of the strike, only the sketchiest reports filtered through to the West—little more than rumors really. Years later we learned the horrifying details from Aleksandr Solzhenitsyn and other dissidents who had interviewed eyewitnesses or people knowledgeable about the uprising. But even today all but a very few Soviet citizens remain ignorant of what happened in Novocherkassk, of the fact that their government dispatched troops and tanks to shoot down unarmed workers.

The histories of the democratic nations are not without their share of violent labor strife and injustices against working people. Few nations among the democracies have experienced as violent a history of labor relations as the United States, where efforts to organize coal mines, steel mills, automobile plants, and other industries resulted in many injuries and even deaths to workers and union activists. The difference between the experiences of workers in the U.S. and those, for example, in the Soviet Union, is that the sacrifices of American workers have produced change and reform, while in the Soviet Union worker revolts have evoked harsh retribution. In the U.S. newspapers carry extensive coverage of labor disputes; in most Communist nations labor unrest is ignored by the government-controlled media. In the West the leaders of working class struggles have been made the heroes of a whole popular culture; in Communist countries strike leaders today are often shipped off to mental hospitals or labor camps. In the West public outrage over labor abuse has led to important changes in government policy, changes which ultimately brought about the legitimization of trade unions. In the Communist world, on the other hand, official trade unions continue to operate as docile servants of the party and state and are, not surprisingly, regarded with contempt by the workers themselves.

Some will respond that even today the lot of workers in the West is far from perfect: all industrial democracies suffer from the phenomenon known as stagflation, characterized by simultaneous increases in the rates of inflation and unemployment. The democracies also face problems caused by the recent influx of migrant workers. The rights of unions to organize public employees remains unsettled in some countries, including the United States. There is, as well, the relatively recent challenge to the American labor movement posed by a resurgence in anti-union sentiments among employers who increasingly resort to the use of lawyers, public relations experts, industrial psychologists, and personnel managers in an effort to prevent trade union organization of their businesses.

But as the authors of this study make clear, a distinction must be made between labor rights and labor problems. There are many unsolved labor problems in democratic societies, but labor rights are well established in law and exercised as a matter of course. In Communist countries labor problems are present too, although frequently hidden or denied, but labor rights are suppressed with the same zealous wholeheartedness as are other human rights. There is, in fact, much evidence to suggest that worker dissidents are dealt with even more severely (at least in the Soviet Union) than are dissidents with intellectual, religious, or artistic roots. The organizers of free trade union movements have been sent to mental hospitals in both the Soviet Union and Rumania, while in these and other Communist countries the authorities have gone to great lengths to demonstrate that worker protest is either the product of mental aberration or that worker dissidents are little more than common criminals attempting to camouflage their lawbreaking by posing as dissenters. In the latter regard, we have seen a number of recent instances where worker dissidents have been charged not with political offenses ("anti-regime propaganda," "slander against the state," and so on) but rather with transparently fabricated criminal violations.

Despite the persecution suffered by worker dissidents in the Soviet bloc, little attention has been devoted to the worker question by individuals or organizations active in the human rights cause, including those specially concerned with repression in the Communist world. When human rights agendas are drawn up, they far too often fail to include such issues as the right to organize trade unions independent of government or party control, the right to strike, and the right to bargain collectively, even though each of these rights is recognized as fundamental in international law.

All this may change in the wake of the 1980 Polish workers' revolt, particularly since the principal demand of the workers—for free trade unions—is really a human rights objective. After Poland, it can no longer be argued that workers have no special human rights concerns; the overwhelming contempt exhibited by the Polish workers for the official party-controlled trade unions is an attitude not limited to Poland. Were it not for the totalitarian ruthlessness in other Eastern bloc countries, the movement for free trade unions would certainly expand beyond Poland's boundaries. But those who believe that trade union and worker issues deserve greater attention from human rights advocates in the West must also overcome certain myths and prejudices about trade unionism which are deeply rooted in the culture of the West, and particularly in the United States. Trade union rights are taken for granted; more significantly, trade union leaders occupy a far-from-exalted position in our mass culture. The union leader is routinely depicted in books, movies, and television programs as venal and corrupt, and unions are presented as bastions of racial and sexual discrimination and retrograde social attitudes.

Another problem, perhaps even more important than the poor image labor unions suffer, is the growing view that free trade unionism is somehow incompatible with economic development, that only the most highly developed industrial democracies can afford the "luxury" of independent unions. This belief is shared by individuals from a cross section of the ideological spectrum: foreign policy specialists, businessmen, and of course, those sympathetic to those forms of authoritarianism adopted under the guise of "socialism." Although the notion that free unions and economic advancement are incompatible is usually raised in connection with the Third World, this view also influences attitudes toward the Eastern bloc. These countries, it is asserted, could not have achieved their level of economic growth or modernization without adopting centrally planned, command economies which tightly control, restrict, and regiment the workforce. Such attitudes, joined with an often-prevailing view that "we really can't do anything" to foster change in Eastern Europe, have hampered the effectiveness of human rights advocates in addressing an issue which is not only fundamental to human rights, but could play the pivotal role in a movement for reform in the Communist world.

It should be noted that the traditional definition of trade union rights—in which such concepts as freedom of association, the right to strike, and free collective bargaining are integral—is the accepted standard in international law. The conventions adopted by the International Labor Organization, and duly ratified by the Soviet Union and its satellites, make no reference to the "leading role of the party," the "moral obligation to work," "proletarian internationalism," or any of the other concepts that are peculiar to Communist trade union policy, and in fact, they explicitly rule out many of the anti-worker policies carried out by Communist countries.

The major purpose of this study is to inject the issue of worker rights into the broader human rights debate. When plans for the study were being discussed, no one anticipated that within a year's time the workers of a major Communist country would have achieved a degree of trade union autonomy unprecedented in the Communist world. The actions of the Polish workers, however, clearly support the premise underlying this study: that workers throughout the world want trade unions which they themselves organize, participate in, and control, and that they perceive of trade unions as forces for the liberation of men and women, rather than as institutions designed to keep workers under party, state, or for that matter, corporate control. Clearly, these aspirations are infectious, and in the coming period the demands for increased worker freedom and trade union autonomy will become a crucial issue of democratic rights. Nor will this struggle be limited to Eastern Europe: workers throughout the world, especially in countries where industrialization is proceeding at an accelerated pace, will no doubt find inspiration from the Polish example.

This study, then, is but a beginning. The demands of working people for a role of real influence in the decisions which determine their work lives, their standard of living, and their political and social rights present a major challenge to the world. We believe that this study conveys a sense of the kinds of democratic institutions which workers can create if allowed to function under conditions of democracy. It also reveals how the machinery of totalitarian repression can transform institutions conceived in democratic ideals into institutions which are at best irrelevant to the needs of workers and at worst destructive of their interests. Hopefully, this study will encourage those committed to human rights to focus their attention and energies on a question that is crucial to the future prospects of democracy.

Workers' Rights in Western Industrial Countries

By Adolph Sturmthal

Introduction

> If it is true as I assume that pressures toward inequality and status ascription are basic to human society, then it follows that those who would reduce such reactions as much as possible must seek for institutionalized means of restraining them. And I know of no means to do so which are superior to or even approach the method of conflict. The only groups which have an "interest" to modify and reduce inequality are the underprivileged. But the underprivileged can impress their concerns on the social system only in a polity in which they are free to organize in unions, parties, cooperatives, and the like. *The only effective restraint on the power of the dominant class is counter-power.* The primary weapons of the lower strata, of the exploited classes, are the ability to organize, to strike, to demonstrate, and to vote rulers out of office. In any given society at any given time in history, the lower classes may not use these weapons effectively, they may not recognize their interests, but there is no other way. Hence a society which denies the masses such rights is not only undemocratic politically, it also fosters the increased privileges of the ruling groups. As Milovan Djilas and many others have demonstrated, Communist dictatorship has meant the creation of a "New Class" more exploitative than the ruling classes of Western capitalism. The distribution of rewards in the Soviet Union is much more unequal than it is in most other industrialized nations. And it is primarily the fear of the potentially revolutionary masses that has, since 1953, led the rulers of the Eastern European states to make concessions to alleviate the standard of living of the workers and peasants.
>
> —Seymour Martin Lipset, *Political Man, The Social Bases of Politics.*

However, concessions made unilaterally and out of fear are no substitute for rights established in law or custom, whose observation the beneficiaries are entitled to claim and enforce by the procedures guaranteed by a free society: by strikes, demonstrations, organizing, votes, or in the courts. It is in this spirit that the International Labor Organization enacted not only Conventions 87 and 98 laying down the right to freedom of association and to free collective bargaining, but also the convention forbidding the use of forced labor, the convention on the protection of workers' representatives, the convention on trade union rights in the public services, and so on.

It is in the light of these principles that the following brief explorations of trade union rights in a number of democratic industrial countries are undertaken. Particular stress is placed on four main issues: (1) the workers' right to organize; (2) their right to engage in collective bargaining on wages, fringe benefits, and working conditions; (3) their right to withhold their labor—i.e., their right to strike; (4) their right to engage in political activities.

Needless to say, these rights are complementary. They are also elementary rights without which the welfare of the worker depends upon the arbitrariness or good will of the employer and state. Without these rights a democratic state cannot exist. We would, rather, be left, at best, with a benevolent despotism, at worst, with a system of dictatorial oppression.

The United Kingdom

The outstanding example of the free development of trade union organization and union action in the West is Great Britain, the country in which collective bargaining first developed. It has often been described as the "home of collective bargaining."

However, as Allan Flanders put it in his article "Great Britain" (in *Contemporary Collective Bargaining in Seven Countries,* edited by Adolf Sturmthal), "for a long time this child of industrialism remained unwanted and unloved." Trade unions had to overcome considerable resistance, less from the state than from employers. But by the end of the nineteenth century, trade unionism and collective bargaining were well established among skilled craftsmen—primarily but not exclusively in the engineering, shipbuilding, and printing industries—and the less skilled piece-rate workers in the textile and shoe industries. The development of modern collective bargaining passed through a stage of trade union-established "working rules" for the first group and so-called standard price lists for the piece workers. These distinctions disappeared when collective bargaining became an accepted practice. The Trade Disputes Act of 1906 removed all legal obstacles to the industrial activities of the unions, completing a process that began with the Trade Union Act of 1871. Moreover, legislation such as the Conciliation Act of 1896 indicated government approval for the principle of free collective bargaining and reduced the role of the government to that of a mediator in industrial conflicts. Further legislation was designed to encourage collective bargaining in industries where management resisted engaging in negotiations with the unions or where unions were inadequately organized. "State power was used... during this period [the first two decades of this century] both to promote the growth of collective bargaining and to make good some of its inadequacies," wrote Flanders in "Great Britain."

World War I brought about a growth of trade unions, a shift to national bargaining, and a temporary use of compulsory arbitration to prevent strikes, without, however, making strikes illegal. Immediately after the end of hostilities Britain returned to a system of voluntarism by offering the facilities of an Industrial Court, whose awards were not binding, for the solution of disputes. Only when World War II broke out were restrictions on the right to strike reintroduced. Order 1305 provided for compulsory arbitration but left a loophole making strikes legal if the minister of labor did not take action within three weeks after the conflict had been reported to him. At the same time the order made it obligatory for all employers to observe terms of employment no less favorable than those contained in the collective agreements of the trade in the district of the employer. Order 1305 functioned so well, and the economic distress of England after World War II was so severe, that the order outlasted the war by several years. But a reaction against legal procedures against striking workers in 1950 made the repeal of the penal prosecution of strikes and lockouts inevitable. What survived was voluntary arbitration as a last resort. In the industries where unions were too weak to engage in effective collective bargaining, national minimum wage rates were set by the government through so-called Wage Councils which could also suggest standards for minimum working conditions. The expectation was that these councils would abandon their functions as soon as strong unions emerged in the particular industries, such as hotels and restaurants (catering) and retail trade.

The nationalization of some industries following the end of World War II had little impact on bargaining procedures and the freedom of unions to strike, affiliate with the Labor Party, and so on. In most of these industries, well-established bargaining relationships with powerful unions were simply maintained. Perhaps the main change was that bargaining was now extended to all non-manual workers as well. Even professional employees followed the example of their colleagues in manual occupations by organizing and bargaining with their employers.

British agreements are often nationwide in scope, providing frequently for special "London Supplements" to take account of the high cost of living in the capital. However, the national agreements are commonly supplemented by shop agreements, frequently of an informal nature, concluded by shop stewards elected in the plants. Since typically several unions organizing different—and sometimes the same—class of workers operate in a plant or enterprise, shop-steward committees are formed for bargaining purposes. Shop stewards, originally an alternative form of workers' representation directly elected by the workers in the plants, were incorporated into the trade unions after World War I. They achieved a high degree of independence from the unions during and after World War II. Because individual stewards are responsible for more than one union, the committees are free of the control of any single union, a fact which has occasionally led to contradictory policies between unions and stewards. Since grievances are also in the hands of the stewards, the stewards have become, especially since World War II, the most important bargaining agent for the worker in the shop. (This and related facts have caused the Donovan Commission to speak of a double system of bargaining in the U.K. consisting of national agreements concluded by the unions and of the far more important formal or informal plant understandings arranged by the stewards.)

A further complication of the British industrial relations system is that different unions sometimes attempted to organize the same group of workers. This has led to numerous jurisdictional disputes involving two or three unions. Finally, the Trades Union Congress (TUC)—significantly, not the government—stepped in and devised procedures to settle internal disputes. This system (the "Bridlington agreement") has worked relatively well.

There are thus no limits on the right to organize, to engage in collective bargaining, and—apart from wartime emergencies—to engage in strikes. An attempt by the Conservative government in 1971 to break with the tradition of governmental nonintervention and to regulate some aspects of industrial relations by legislation was defeated by the concerted refusal of most of the unions to cooperate.

As for political action, the basic fact is that the Labor Party was the creation of the unions and to this day depends largely on their financial contributions for its operation. The traditional procedure consisted of union members paying the "political levy" unless they declared in writing their unwillingness to do so ("contracting out"). After the unsuccessful general strike of 1926 a Conservative government reversed this rule: the union member had to state in writing his willingness to pay a contribution for political action ("contracting in"). The Labor government that took office in 1945 returned to the earlier procedure, with the result that the proportion of union members paying the political levy rose sharply. Apart from this one incident, there has been no government interference in the political activities of unions.

The settlement of industrial disputes is a voluntary procedure. Arbitration is sometimes agreed upon by the bargaining participants to set the terms of an agreement, though it is rarely used to determine the interpretation or application of a contract—the reverse of the common United States practice. What is important is that, except in wartime—these procedures are accepted voluntarily by both sides.

As a result of the dual system of collective bargaining, the agreements themselves fall into two main classes: national and regional contracts on the one hand, plant agreements on the other. Neither has legal validity, in the sense that neither can be enforced by the courts, but both are commonly observed in good faith as they are the "many uncodified practices accepted by employer and trade unions alike, often but not exclusively confined to particular establishments, which are virtually the subject of unwritten agreements," as Flanders observed in "Great Britain." Among such unwritten agreements are institutions such as closed shops and union shops which, Flanders continued, make the union card "the key to employment in many skilled trades.... Employers turn to the unions in the first place to help them fill their vacancies." While seniority rules regarding layoffs and rehiring are rarely written into agreements, they also belong among the unwritten understandings in many, though not all, large industries.

The result of all this is a highly unsystematic and sometimes even inconsistent picture Flanders described as "knitted together, if not by any consistent theory, at least by certain common assumptions...good industrial relations are best created by voluntary action." This article of faith has at times been challenged by the labor-market tension produced by prolonged full employment, a situation which tended to foster imports, while the improvement of exports following enlarged production manifested itself only with some time lag. Another consequence was the upward pressure on money wages resulting from the imbalance on the labor market. Inflation and balance-of-payments crises enhanced by the loss of overseas investments hampered economic expansion: stop-and-go policies became the order of the day.

Full employment and inflation thus became the main challenges to the kind of free collective bargaining that characterizes British industrial relations. The problems were rendered more difficult by what Lord Beveridge in his classic study "Full Employment in a Free Society" called competitive sectional bargaining. The Trades

Union Congress has no control over the bargaining tactics and objectives of its affiliated unions, and not all unions are affiliated with the TUC. Individual unions and, as we have seen, shop stewards carry on their bargaining activities on their own, often motivated by a desire to obtain better results for their members than other unions with which they feel they are in competition. These "coercive comparisons," as they have come to be known, result in the advantages obtained by one union or steward spreading to related firms and industries, in ever-widening circles.

During World War II and for a period after 1945 the unions accepted wage restraint, but by 1949-50 resistance had grown to the point where the General Council of the TUC in June 1950 abandoned further efforts to induce union restraint and left policy determination to "the good sense and reasonableness which have been displayed by unions...." Subsequent history has been marked by repeated attempts to bring wages under some form of voluntary control, with differing results. In general Labor governments, thanks to their close relations with the unions, have had a slightly better record than the Conservatives, but in the end, i.e., in the late 1970s, even the Labor government of James Callaghan met overwhelming union resistance to control from above. Moreover, given the influence of shop stewards on effective wage rates and earnings, the unions are not at all certain that they can actually control the rate of increase of many wages. What remains is moral suasion, whose effectiveness is widely questioned, at least for the long run. Thus even in the present difficulties that Britain is facing, the unions are maintaining their fundamental freedom from governmental control. However, it is an open question whether collective bargaining can long remain a private arrangement between labor and management alone, or whether the government in some way will enter the scene as well. Nor is it obvious to what extent full employment or other fundamental factors are responsible for inflation, especially since 1967 when unemployment and prices rose at the same time. This phenomenon, termed *stagflation*, also observed in the U.S. and other Western industrial nations, has not yet undergone insightful analysis, and even less successful solution.

The United States

Until the 1930s the American labor movement—the American Federation of Labor (A.F.L.)—represented no more than three million workers, i.e., one out of sixteen workers. This changed radically and rapidly in the 1930s as a result of several main events: the Great Depression, the emergence of the New Deal, the passage of the National Labor Relations Act of 1935, and the establishment of the Congress of Industrial Organizations (CIO).

The law of 1935 for the first time gave workers government protection in their efforts to form unions. As Neil W. Chamberlain explained in "Collective Bargaining in the U.S." (in *Contemporary Collective Bargaining in Seven Countries,* edited by Adolf Sturmthal), workers now had the right to call for a secret vote to determine whether they wished to be represented by a union, and if so, which one. If a majority voted for a particular union, it was given exclusive rights to bargain on behalf of that group of workers, and the employer was required by law to negotiate with the union in good faith to arrive at an agreement which had to be set down in writing. Employers were forbidden to interfere with union organization, although they were later given the right to present their point of view to their employees.

The second development was the effort of a number of former member organizations of the American Federation of Labor to set up industrial unions representing unskilled or semiskilled workers, and to disregard the jurisdictional rights of the AFL unions. The inevitable conflict led to the organization of two rival federations, the AFL and the CIO. Their competition for the allegiance of the workers contributed to a considerable increase in union organization and improvements in wages and working conditions. Organized labor emerged as one of the main power centers of the country, even though the percentage of the labor force that joined unions remained relatively small when compared with that of other countries, ranging from slightly more than one-third, and most of the time standing at about one-fourth.

While the Great Depression of the 1930s did not significantly alter the AFL's acceptance of capitalism, other major changes did occur. The first fundamental change occurred in 1932—prior to the advent of the New Deal—with the passage of the Norris-

La Guardia Act. This act outlawed the so-called yellow-dog contract which prevented workers who were hired under that contract from joining unions and also protected strikes and picketing in labor disputes against court injunctions (temporary court orders) as long as these activities were carried on lawfully, i.e., without violence. This relieved organized labor at long last of the threat of court interference with normal union activities.

The next instrument with which the government—now headed by Franklin D. Roosevelt—encouraged the growth of labor unions, was, as mentioned, the National Labor Relations Act, also called the Wagner Act, which was and, in spite of modification, still is the pillar on which American labor rests. In addition to guaranteeing the workers the right to unionize and bargain if the majority of a particular workers' group so wishes, the law protects the workers against unfair labor practices by the employer. Interference with the right to unionize and to bargain, attempts to dominate a union, discrimination because of union membership, or reprisals against an employee for testifying before the National Labor Relations Board which supervises the administration and application of the act, and finally, refusal to bargain in good faith with the union designated by the majority of the employees are forbidden by the act. Amendments enacted in 1947, twelve years after the original law was passed, provided penalties for unfair practices on the part of the union for protection of those who did not wish to join a union, for forcing an employer to engage in discriminatory hiring practices, for engaging in violence while picketing, and so on. However, a union-shop agreement was declared legal. Under it, an employee may be forced to join a union after thirty days of employment and may lose his job for nonpayment of union dues. This is different from a closed shop, which requires that a worker be a union member before he can be hired.

The government regulatory procedures leading to union recognition and the conclusion of a collective agreement provide legal protection to serve the process of collective bargaining rather than to hinder it. In any case, the government does not dictate or influence the content of such agreements—except on the basis of special authorization in carefully defined national emergencies such as World War II, the Korean War, and a short period in 1971 in connection with a balance-of-payments crisis. Special agencies are established to handle these problems while the National Labor Relations Board (NLRB) continues to function. The only major exception to all this is the setting of a minimum wage by the government to prevent the exploitation of weakly organized or unorganized groups of workers.

A crucial issue involved in NLRB procedures is the determination of the bargaining unit. While most collective-bargaining agreements cover the employees of a single enterprise or plant, and are negotiated by the management of that plant rather than an employer's association, the NLRB may designate smaller bargaining units, based on the bargaining history of a group of workers, community of interests, special skills, or other considerations. Once again, the Board merely sets the framework for bargaining; it does not influence the content of the agreement. Nevertheless results in one unit may influence the outcome in another. Thus Professor Arthur Ross, in his *Trade Union Wage Policy*, has spoken of "orbits of coercive comparisons" which relate to occupations, industries, or areas with which workers traditionally compare their own earnings. This phenomenon leads to "wage rounds," where certain contracts play a pattern-setting role that others follow. The degree of influence that unions exert in any market economy on setting real wage rates is still a matter of dispute among labor economists. There is, however, no disagreement that government has little influence apart from periods of severe national emergency (and the setting of the minimum wage).

One further major piece of legislation resulted from an outburst of strikes following the restraint that organized labor had accepted—though with some notable exceptions—during World War II.

The new law reflected not only reaction to strikes, but also a reluctance of many employers to accept what they regarded as the pro-labor bias of the Wagner Act. Although President Truman vetoed the Taft-Hartley Act, Congress, with a two-thirds majority as the Constitution requires, overrode his veto.

The law—established to counteract sections of the Wagner Act—prohibited unions from coercing workers into joining unions. Just as the Wagner Act provided for elections by which the workers could decide whether they wanted to be represented by a union, the new law established "decertification" elections. The closed shop was now expressly forbidden, but continued in fact in some industries such as printing, building, seafaring, and maritime with the active cooperation of the employers, as Lloyd Ulman pointed out in "Unionism and Collective Bargaining in the Modern Period" (in *American Economic History*, by Seymour E. Harris). Ulman stated that the act originally provided that "union shops [where workers have to join the union after having been hired] could not be authorized unless the majority of all the employees in the bargaining unit concerned voted in favor of the union shop; this provision reflected the drafters' assumption that many workers acquiesced in union-security provisions only under duress. However, the union shop won in 97.1 percent of the 46,119 separate elections held between August 1947 and October 1951 (and it won 84.8 percent of the votes cast)...and this provision was subsequently repealed." The "secondary boycott," directed against a neutral employer, to force him to cease dealing with employers with whom the union had a dispute, was also outlawed. Jurisdictional disputes—i.e., disputes among unions over which members should be given a work assignment—were to be settled by the NLRB if the unions could not reach agreement within ten days.

As to strikes creating "national emergencies," the law contains a whole list of tried and untried remedies to delay a strike of this kind. Failing all else, the President is empowered to call on Congress "for consideration and appropriate action." Thus a strike can be postponed, but not outlawed, unless Congress enacts special legislation whose contitutionality would have to withstand examination by the Supreme Court. In fact, this kind of special legislation has never been used. President Truman's intervention in the steel conflict of 1952 was based on the power of the presidency, a claim that the Supreme Court rejected. In some individual states which have jurisdiction over workers whose product or services do not pass state lines, more effective anti-union legislation has been enacted, but Supreme Court decisions have taken the sting out of many of these laws. The main exception was the declaration that "right-to-work" laws, forbidding union-security clauses, were constitutional if enacted by a state.

No government regulations—except the election procedures of the NLRB to establish a bargaining agent by majority vote—affected the inner workings of unions until 1959, when the Labor-Management Reporting and Disclosure Act was passed. Prior to this, the unions themselves had adopted a number of self-regulating procedures, beginning in 1949 when nine affiliated organizations of the CIO were expelled because of Communist domination. This, together with the increased political interest of the AFL after the passage of the Taft-Hartley Act in 1947, brought the AFL and the CIO nearer to each other. The CIO had established a political action committee in 1944, and the deaths of the presidents of the two rival federations, William Green (AFL) and Philip Murray (CIO), removed some of the personal hindrances standing in the way of a merger of the two organizations, which took place in 1955.

An important development was an internal cleansing process over the issue of corruption. The AFL, even before the merger, had expelled the International Longshoremen's Association. The new AFL-CIO constitution pledged the federation "to protect the labor movement from any and all corrupt influences." The executive council, by two-thirds vote, could suspend any affiliate for corruption or Communist influence. In short order, the Teamsters, the Laundry Workers, and the Bakers were expelled by a convention of the AFL-CIO on the recommendation of the council.

The legislation of 1959 reinforced the anti-corruption efforts of the unions, but at the same time introduced a measure of federal intervention in the internal affairs of labor beyond what the unions wished. A bill of rights for union members was created, internal union election procedures were regulated, limits were established on the control of national officers over local unions, and reporting and disclosure requirements were established. In the process, the law tended to eliminate whatever racial discrimination against some union members continued to exist in some unions.

The main task of unions is not simply to negotiate and write a contract, but—perhaps still more important—to administer it and to settle individual worker or group grievances that arise under the agreement. The grievance procedure, usually set out in great detail, is in many ways the core of the contract. Rather complicated procedures have been worked out providing for up to seven appeal stages. Quite commonly impartial umpires are the last court of appeals. In every case, they are chosen by agreement of the two parties and paid in equal parts by them. Their job is not to write a contract, but to decide disputes about its application or interpretation. Unions maintain a large number of full-time employees whose job it is to proceed from one plant to another and to intervene in the grievance process if the complaint has not been settled at a lower level by the elected shop steward. It is the shop steward and the full-time "international representative" who are in most cases the union officials with whom the rank and file has the most direct and frequent contact. The union has free access to the plant and is indeed regarded as a counterpart to management. Even though only a relatively small part of the labor force is organized, the unionized sector exerts considerable influence on the entire industrial relations system. In some cases bargaining has become a more or less continuous process so that difficult problems can be explored long before the expiration date of the contract.

One last characteristic of U.S. bargaining deserves to be noted. The typical collective agreement is elaborate, running sometimes over more than one hundred printed pages, and quite complex. The agreements refer to "the scope of the bargaining unit, contract duration, strikes and lockouts, union security, management rights, grievance procedures, wages (rates, incentive systems, job classification, etc.), work rules, hours of work, discipline and discharge, paid and unpaid leave, employee benefit plans, and the role of seniority in layoffs, promotions, and transfers, as Donald E. Cullen explained in his "Recent Trends in Collective Bargaining in the United States," (in *Collective Bargaining in Industrialized Market Economies,* published by the International Labor Organization). The rapid growth of fringe benefits embodied in collective agreements, while the official Social Security System is based on legislation, has further expanded the size of the agreements.

New problems have arisen as a result of government-sponsored "incomes policies," intended to restrain inflation. None of these has so far had a long life, and none has operated with success without the cooperation of the unions. Their willingness to accept such efforts has usually been made contingent on their direct participation in their administration, when the policies required an administrative apparatus, and upon the inclusion of other-than-wages forms of income in the regulations.

France

Collective bargaining became generalized in France on a significant scale in 1936, the year of Leon Blum's Popular Front government. It is true that collective-bargaining agreements were concluded before World War I and to a greater extent after 1918 when the unions, until then opposed to collective bargaining as contradicting their class-struggle principles, finally declared it "a profound error to see in collective agreements a form of collaboration (between employers and unions)." But these agreements, mostly reached on the basis of a law passed in 1919, were few in number and covered only a small fraction of the labor force.

The main problem was the weakness of the unions. Although the freedom to organize unions was recognized in 1884, the unions enrolled only a small elite of skilled workers, most of whom were dedicated to the ideas of revolutionary syndicalism, a philosophy which rejected both capitalism and Marxian socialism. The latter had most of its appeal among the coalminers of the North and the heavy industry in the St. Etienne area. It was only during World War I, when heavy industry replaced the small artisan shop in the Paris suburbs, that Marxian ideas became dominant among the workers of the Paris area at the expense of syndicalism.

After 1918, under the impact of the Russian Revolution, the left wing of the Socialist Party, supported by the remnants of the syndicalist movement, formed the Communist Party. For some time it remained vastly inferior in numbers and parliamentary representation to the Socialists, emerging as a major factor in French national politics only in 1936, when it formed part of the Popular Front movement which made the Socialist leader Leon Blum prime minister.

In the same year, a new foundation for collective bargaining was established, and for one or two years, trade union membership grew at an amazing pace, as did the number and the scope of collective agreements. World War II interrupted this process, and it was only in 1950 that a new departure became possible.

At that time French trade unionism was split along ideological and religious lines into three main currents: the old Confederation Generale du Travail (CGT), dominated by the CP; the smaller

Force Ouvrière, a mixture of socialism and business unionism; and the Christian unions, in the process of freeing themselves from church dominance (partly because the upper ranks of the church hierarchy were regarded as guilty of having collaborated with the Nazis during the occupation by German troops). A fourth confederation, that of the *Cadres,* organized the upper ranks of the white-collar classes and was less tied than the others to a particular political party.

The law of 1950 designated some—later almost all—unions as "most representative" and entitled to engage in organizing, bargaining, and with a few exceptions, striking. Agreements could be national, regional, or local in scope, but in practice national agreements proved to be the most frequent and important. Plant or enterprise agreements were concluded in a small number of rather large corporations.

The characteristics of French collective bargaining were and remain the unlimited freedom of unions to organize employees with the result that several competitive unions often coexist in the same plant. The minister of labor may extend all or part of a collective agreement to workers and employers not represented at the bargaining table and not partners to the agreement, giving the agreement the force of law. A minimum wage for all occupations and industries—differing here from the British pattern—is prepared by a government-appointed Higher Commission on Collective Agreements and enacted by the government itself. For nationalized enterprises, the law provides two alternatives: where the nationalized enterprises form only a part of an entire industry, they are subject to the same procedures and the same national agreement as the private sector of the industry; where all or almost all of an industry is nationalized, special procedures are provided which are subject to fairly frequent change. The most important provision empowered the minister responsible for the industry in question to determine the total sum available for wage improvements or changes in working conditions—subject to confirmation by the minister of finance—and then leave it to collective bargaining between the "most representative unions" and the management of the industry to arrange for the distribution of the total among the different categories of employees.

The right to strike was made universal, according to the Constitution, "within the framework of laws which regulate it."

In fact only strikes of policemen—though they could unionize—and acts of sabotage on work for national defense were specifically prohibited, and the prohibition was enacted only after long hesitation. Conciliation efforts were made compulsory; arbitration, voluntary.

However, collective bargaining is less significant in France than legislation and administrative action. This relates not only to substantive questions such as the minimum wage discussed above, but also to the institutions of the industrial relations system itself. Thus not only must the "most representative" unions be designated by the minister, who also decides about the extension of agreements; works' councils *(comites d'éntreprise)*, representing the workers in a plant and an enterprise and handling primarily their welfare institutions, were created by decree or law, as were the *"délégués du personnel"* (shop stewards handling individual complaints of employees). However, the membership of these institutions is designated by the workers themselves, with the participation of the unions.

Thus, while the government plays a large role in the industrial relations systems, it is important to remember that it is a freely elected government, that the right to strike is almost unlimited, that the workers' representatives are designated by the employees themselves, and that the unions are free to engage in political action subject only to the limitations imposed by tradition or their own statutes. In fact, the largest trade union confederation, the Confederation Generale du Travail, is Communist-controlled and frequently used for the purposes of Communist Party policies. A more important limitation on trade union influences is the numerical and financial weakness of French unions, magnified by the various splits of the labor organizations which are, as a rule, confronted by unified employers' organizations at the bargaining table.

Major changes were later adopted mainly as a result of political developments that exerted pressures upon the government and employers. Of special importance here was the mass eruption of 1968, which led to the Grenelle "statement" (*constat*), named after the street on which the Ministry of Social Affairs is located. This agreement provided for negotiations between the National Employers' Council and the various trade union confederations. The main results were an expansion of the issues covered by collective agreements (hours of work, salaried status of workers, profit-sharing) and the conclusion of agreements on employment (regulating layoffs), on vocational training, and perhaps most important in the long run, on the free access of unions to the workplace. One consequence of these changes was the far more frequent conclusion of plantwide agreements. One of the difficulties standing in the way of a more rapid growth of the latter is the fact that French employers most frequently leave bargaining to their trade associations and have little experience in bargaining themselves. Thus in practice plant agreements have been limited to very large enterprises. The example of Italy—and, to a lesser extent, West Germany—shows, however, that this difficulty can be overcome, for example, by the use of employer-association representatives in the negotiations of individual enterprises.

Perhaps the main hindrance to further developments in collective bargaining is the reluctance of some of the unions, especially those of the Communist-led CGT, to engage without reservation in collective bargaining. Often, this is merely a "symbolic" refusal to sign an agreement without any attempt to defeat it. In this case, the CGT refers to bargaining as "a device to spread the ideology of class collaboration." This forces other unions to stress that signing an agreement should not be interpreted as "integration into the capitalist society." A further consequence of this is the strict refusal of most French unions to accept limitations on their right to strike, even during the period when a contract is in effect.

West Germany

The observer of industrial relations in West Germany is struck by a number of special features: the orderliness of the system; the absence or at least extreme rarity of industrial conflicts; the relative independence of the unions from political parties, so different from the past; the unity of the union movement; the absence of compulsory arbitration; and finally the system of codetermination. To a considerable extent, these features stem from the fact that the system had to be rebuilt from the ruins left by the downfall of the Nazi regime.

Both unions and employers' associations arose slowly after the end of World War II. When unions were gradually formed, at first on a local and state level, finally in a confederation embracing the three Western occupation zones (the East under Soviet control went its own way), they asked the occupation authorities to allow the formation of employers' associations since the unions were used to establishing uniform contract terms by way of multi-employer bargaining and the discipline of the employers' associations was traditionally very strict.

The unions, once their freedom of association was granted by the occupation authorities in the three Western zones, organized on the basis of sixteen—later seventeen—industrial unions combining the membership of the former "free" (i.e., socialist) unions and the Christian unions. This reflected an important lesson drawn from the collapse of the divided unions in the face of the Hitler threat. A small splinter Christian union, mainly in the Sarre district, remained outside the federation. The Communists, rejected by practically the entire working class, could safely be neglected.

The new unions were multi-industrial unions, the largest of which was and remains the Metalworkers' Union (I.G. Metall). The German Labor Confederation, the DGB (Deutscher Gewerkschaftsbund), headquartered in Dusseldorf, is a powerful organization with a full-time elected executive committee of nine members and a large staff, though gradually power has shifted to the individual unions. A special white-collar union is not affiliated with the DBG, and conflicts do occasionally arise when DBG unions try, not entirely without success, to enroll the white-collar workers of their respective industries. That the civil servants stayed out of the DGB is almost a matter of course in the status-conscious society which Germany remains in spite of the sharp democratization process following the defeat in World War II. Another characteristic of the movement is the heavy concentration of power at the top of the organizational pyramid, a trend reinforced by the absence, until recently, of active union groups in the plants. The works' councils, elected by all workers in a given plant, though consisting overwhelmingly of union members, are formally independent of the unions. They conclude agreements supplementary to those reached by the unions and handle grievances. But as institutions legally committed to "industrial peace," the councils cannot organize strikes, though they have considerable rights—enhanced by a law of 1972—of codetermination or at least consultation on working conditions, job evaluation, working hours, compensation for those laid off, and so forth.

The main contracts are concluded by the national or district unions, often with regional scope. The master contract *(Manteltarif)* is usually brief, since it covers only very broad questions that apply to all enterprises concerned. This is supplemented by a wage agreement and a separate salary agreement for the white-collar employees. The works' council agreement regulating the council activities and expenses and supplementing (improving) the wages and conditions of the union contract, has already been mentioned. The council may also conclude a plant-rules agreement concerning shift hours, attendance rules, welfare facilities, and the like, which forms part of the package, as do understandings about vacations, arbitration, and similar matters.

The wages set in the multienterprise (national or regional) agreement represent a kind of minimum wage. Such agreements serve as a basis for supplementary understandings (without legal validity, but almost always observed) by the works' council or by individual workers. Especially during the long period of labor shortage, the gap between contract and effective rates—just as in England—tended to be considerable. The importance of the contract wage *as a minimum* is enhanced by the authority of the minister to "extend" the contract to firms and workers that are not members of their respective organizations, provided the contracting employers' organization represents firms employing more than half of the workers in the industry concerned. It is thus the degree of organization in the employers' association, rather than the union, which is crucial.

The low level of industrial conflict in West Germany is

remarkable; it is surpassed only by neighboring Austria and Switzerland. Any number of reasons have been cited in explanation of this phenomenon: fear of unemployment that ravaged Germany during most of the life of the Weimar Republic and greatly contributed to the Nazi victory; union lack of self-confidence after the collapse of labor's resistance to the rising tide of national socialism; later, the rapid recovery of Germany after 1945, permitting equally rapidly rising incomes; and finally widespread understanding that in spite of Marshall Plan aid, consumption had to be restrained in order to devote resources to the reconstruction of the war-devastated productive apparatus, a view shared, of course, by the powerful employers' association and for a long time by the conservative government. Later, when the Social Democrats under Willy Brandt entered the government, the "concerted action" was created, an informal get-together of government, employers, union leaders, and academic experts who attempted, usually with some measure of success, to develop strategies to achieve increases in real incomes without conflict. Although interrupted by a dispute on codetermination, concerted action has resumed its operations in a slightly changed form and greatly contributes to the low degree of inflation and the low frequency of strikes in West Germany. It must be noted, however, that strikes are perfectly legal and that in fact important strike movements did exist in 1969 and again ten years later. The infrequency of strikes is a purely voluntary phenomenon. Compulsory arbitration is completely absent from the system.

Since they emerged from a merger between former Socialist and Christian trade unionists, the unions are no longer directly tied to any political party. Yet since the great majority of the trade unionists support the Social Democrats (SPD), the presidents of the DGB and of all affiliated unions are Socialists, while one of the DGB vice presidents belongs to the Christian group. The political identities of German unionists are retained and respected. The unions may and do take stands on issues that seem important to them, but they no longer officially support any party directly, though in all essentials union leadership supports the SPD.

An important and new institution of German industrial relations is the system of codetermination. Basically, codetermination calls for the representation of workers and unions on the supervisory boards of share companies. German law provides for a lay supervisory board and a board of full-time managers. The former sets basic policies—in production, sales, and personnel matters—which the managers are to carry out. (In fact, the managers greatly appear to influence the decisions of the supervisory board.)

Codetermination is most far-reaching in the iron and steel industries. There half the members of the supervisory boards represent the workers and other employees as well as the union; the other half represents the shareholders, with an impartial chairman to ensure that a majority decision can be reached. In addition, the enterprise personnel chief, called the labor director, cannot be appointed without approval of the labor members of the supervisory board. Later legislation introduced a modified system into large enterprises in general, leaving out the special procedure for the appointment of the labor director and providing that one of the labor members of the supervisory board was to represent the upper echelons of personnel—a clause that aroused the bitter resistance of the unions. An attempt by the employers to have the entire system thrown out as violation of the constitutional protection of property rights was rejected by the Supreme Court, but the conflict caused the temporary breakup of concerted action.

In smaller companies, employees are represented by two members on the governing board; no such representation exists in the smallest companies. There are, thus, four different systems of managerial organization in existence in West Germany: parity of labor and capital in the iron and coal industry; reduced labor representation as outlined above in the large share companies; representation by two employee delegates in the smaller share companies; no labor representation in all other private enterprises. Combined with the sizable portion of the economy which is state-owned or state-controlled, codetermination gives the German economy the character of a mixed capitalist-socialist society, preserving at the same time a high degree of freedom and social peace.

Experience with worker participation combined with collective bargaining shows that labor influence, though modified by legislated institutions, depends largely on the situation in the labor market which may give or deny power to labor. The favorable in that market has greatly facilitated the technical adjustments in the plants which made West German industry highly competitive in the world markets. This, in turn, has contributed to the favorable employment situation during most of the post-1945 era.

Now that the global economic situation is less favorable, some observers predict that collective bargaining, the main defensive weapon of labor, may take on increased importance. As Gerhard Leminsky wrote in "Worker Participation: The German Experience" (in *Labor Relations in Advanced Industrial Societies: Issues and Problems,* by B. Martin and E. Kassalow), less concern than in the past may be shown for the precise nature of the institutions of the industrial relations system.

Italy

After the Fascist era collective bargaining based on free trade unionism was reintroduced, guaranteed by the Constitution enacted in 1947. The employers were represented by confederations in the largest economic sectors, such as Confindustria and Congragricoltura; on the workers' side, a powerful, unified movement arose which, however, in 1948-49 split into three major labor confederations: CGIL (Confederazione Generale Italiana del Lavoro, under predominantly Communist leadership), CISL (Confederazione Italiana Sindicati dei Lavoratori—Christian with some Socialist cooperation), and UIL (Unione Italiana del Lavoro—Socialist, Social Democratic, and Republican support). These federations are legally entitled to conclude collective agreements; some agreements may be given the force of law and "extended" in the sense in which this term has been used in this study. A presidential decree is required for contracts to be extended.

The foundations for union action were established through high-level agreements immediately following the downfall of the Fascist regime. Some wage problems were also settled at the time in the same way. The conclusion of interconfederal agreements has continued throughout the post-World War II era, but a process of more centralized bargaining set in fairly soon—in the 1950s. In 1954 the national unions obtained the right to negotiate wages. The non-Communist CISL took a further initiative in the direction of plant bargaining, and after a period of opposition and hesitation, the Communist unions (CGIL) followed the same course. An interconfederal agreement gained after the intercession of the minister of labor in 1962 recognized a system of three-tier negotiations: all-sector, national-scope negotiations; national sector negotiations; and plant bargaining.

The enterprise or plant agreements deal with productivity premiums, piecework rates, job evaluation, reduction of hours of work, classification of jobs, and job changes. These agreements greatly restrict managerial authority. They are concluded by "internal commissions" created by an all-sector collective agreement, and not by law as in France and West Germany. These commissions exist in enterprises with more than forty workers "to represent all the workers in their relationship with the direction of the firm." Similar to the German works' council and the French *comité d'entreprise,* they are to "assist in maintaining normal relationships between the workers and the direction of the firm in a spirit of collaboration and mutual understanding to further the regular development of productive activities." However, they are to refer to the trade unions all matters relating to the collective agreement and all disputes that may arise under it.

Alongside the commissions elected by the workers, the unions maintain a network of delegates in the plants whose transfers and layoffs could only be carried out with the approval of the trade unions and the employers' associations. However, the unions had to recognize that they did not have the trained personnel or the training facilities necessary to meet the management experts on a footing of equality. They came to rely more and more on the workers in the plants themselves. In fact, this shift of the responsibility to shop stewards was brought about by spontaneous mass movements in some of the large plants in 1967-68. (See the issue of April/June 1971 of *Sociologie du travail* which is almost exclusively devoted to the Italian developments of that period.)

Ordinarily, the enterprise contracts were concluded by the provincial organizations of the unions whose importance in Italian labor history was traditionally predominant. Together with the union local or without it, they also administered the contracts and organized strikes. However, during the favorable economic situation of the late 1960s the shop stewards *(delegati di reparto)* took over the leadership of the various movements in the plants, pushing aside the internal commissions and the provincial unions. In general, with a few exceptions, this movement was not anti-union, but rather expressed a desire of the rank and file to participate in the action in the workplace. At the same time, the emergence of the shop stewards has contributed to diminishing the ideological divisions within the trade union movement.

The change in the 1970s from a business boom to a much slower economic pace produced a radical change in the labor market.

Unemployment has been one of the most difficult problems for modern Italy, perhaps its most serious challenge. For much of the post-World War II era, great contrasts existed (and continue to exist) between Northern and Central Italy, and the South. Labor shortages prevailed for long periods in the North, while mass unemployment prevailed in the South. Restrictions on dismissals are, therefore, a main union objective. Indeed, after a prolonged struggle, the unions obtained important rights regarding dismissals, both of individuals and of entire groups of employees.

This, of course, did not significantly reduce unemployment. It merely protected the rights of those lucky enough to have jobs, while hundreds of thousands who had just entered the labor market remained unemployed. Real relief came in two ways: mass emigration to neighboring countries whose rapidly expanding economies required additional workers (France, West Germany, Switzerland, and a few others) and the increased demand for labor generated by economic growth. By these developments even some of the excess supply of labor in the most backward part of the country, the area south of Rome and extending all the way to Sicily, was absorbed. By the middle 1960s Northern Italy had emerged as one of the leading industrial areas of Europe. The contrast between the highly efficient industrial organization and the clumsy, slow, and backward administrative machinery of the government led to tensions that at times threatened to break up the social and political fabric of the country. A sizable unemployed intellectual proletariat, assassinations, and kidnappings were warning signals to which the political and social organizations of the country were incapable of responding in time.

From the 1960s onward Italy has endured increased industrial unrest. New young leaders arose, more militant and critical of what their predecessors had done. Moreoever, the astounding economic growth of the country had not been accomplished without creating new problems. The favorable economic situation of the North attracted more than a million workers, mostly moving with their families. Most of them came from the South and possessed few industrial skills. Nevertheless, they usually found jobs in the industrial enterprises of the North which suffered from labor shortages. However, the substructure for this mass immigration, which occurred within a few short years, was lacking. Housing shortages; inadequate urban and suburban transport; "lack of welfare, hospital, and educational facilities manifested themselves, especially in the new centers of industry," wrote Gino Giugni in "Recent Trends in Collective Bargaining in Italy" (in *Collective Bargaining in Industrial Market Economies,* published by the International Labor Organization.) That no legislation on collective bargaining had been enacted, as Article 39 of the Constitution prescribed, was of less importance than the backwardness of the social welfare system.

The governmental machinery proved inadequate to solve these and many other problems. Some of the latter related to the lack of political stability and to the industrial relations system itself. As a result, joint actions of the three confederations became more and more frequent, especially during a wave of unrest in 1969. In the forefront were the metal trade unions of the three confederations which took the lead in a move toward a merger. While earlier talks about this issue remained without concrete action, after 1969 some important results were obtained, though not organic unity. Thus in 1972 formal coordinating machinery was established among the three confederations. This still continues to exist and performs important functions.

The more inefficient the political system became, the more the unions stressed their claim to represent the working class as a whole, and not merely their members. Trade union membership, hard to ascertain partly because membership dues are irregularly paid, is estimated at about half the labor force and thus higher than in many other industrial countries.

One consequence of the enhanced role of the unions was negotiations with the government over issues with only a distant relationship to conventional topics of collective bargaining. Thus the unions "consulted" with the government on questions of social policy, on the government's plans for the advancement of the South, and so forth. As Giugni explained, while the expressions *agreement* and *contract* were carefully avoided, the nature of the discussions was not basically different from negotiations.

Following the French upheaval in 1968, Italy experienced its "hot autumn" of 1969 which involved some four million workers in industry and 1.5 million in agriculture in various strike movements. A "workers' charter" was voted by Parliament in 1970. It guaranteed the workers' right to political freedom at the workplace and removed obstacles to trade union activity in the factory (following in this the U.S. Wagner Act and the French legislation of 1968). Indeed, unions were given facilities in the plant to carry out their work.

The act had great impact on the status of unions. At the request of the unions, nothing was said about their bargaining rights. The unions feared that any legislation on that score would be restrictive. Giugni explained that one of the changes in industrial relations caused by, though not specifically mentioned in, the charter, was the abandonment by government and employers of their stated, but not often observed, refusal to negotiate with the unions while a strike was on. Against the expressed wishes of the employers, plant agreements were concluded in the following years, some supplementing the national agreements, some improving on them. Clearly, traditional management rights are being restricted and the government, in the main, kept out of industrial relations.

Sweden

Sweden has one of the highest rates of trade union organization in the world. About 95 percent of manual workers and 70 percent of white-collar employees in manufacturing belong to unions. Moreover, the Swedish industrial relations system is firmly rooted in the practice of collective bargaining, although collective bargaining in the public sector is of recent date.

The leading trade union organization, LO (Landsorganizationen) represents manual workers. White-collar employees are organized in two main associations: TCO, the Central Organization of Salaried Employees, and SACO, which enrolls professional employees. Employers are primarily organized in the Swedish Employers' Federation (SAF), which speaks for about 25,000 firms in the private economy. The public sector is divided between an organization speaking for the government officers (SAV) and another organization (SFO) which represents nationalized enterprises and was formed in 1970. As elsewhere, the proportion of manual workers and thus of LO members has tended to decline, even though membership has increased in absolute numbers. At the same time, i.e., during the 1960s, TCO more than doubled its membership. Working conditions for members of the two organizations have tended to become more similar, and cooperation between blue- and white-collar unions is not infrequent.

Collective bargaining has been the rule for a long time in Sweden, but the centralized bargaining system which now exists is a product of the mid-1950s. The central agreement between SAF and LO represents a kind of recommendation to their affiliated organizations as to the size of the wage package, recommendations that are practically never disregarded. In this way, the different collective agreements tend to be non-competitive and less inflationary than if they had been, as in the past, concluded independently from each other.

However, while the framework is set in the central agreement, without any government intervention, the different branches conclude their own agreements, as do individual firms. Disputes about the interpretation of an agreement are submitted to higher levels of the organizations and finally settled by a Labor Court or by arbitration if the two parties agree on this procedure.

Issues within the plant are settled by the local union's

representative in the plant in consultation with management. The latter collects union dues.

Central bargaining, just as national agreements in other countries, has run into major difficulties during periods of full employment. While official LO policy has aimed at reducing wage differentials, market forces have tended to increase them during the lifetime of a given contract. "Wage solidarity" as LO policy was officially described, was defeated again and again by the relative scarcity of skilled workers. Moreover, attempts by the LO to extend its contract regulations into more and more details of plant management have been resisted by management representatives on the grounds that they make contracts too elaborate, clumsy, and difficult to understand. A further problem that has arisen in the last few years stems from the desire of the LO to obtain a coordination of all wage negotiations, private and public, manual, white-collar, and professional. This has run into the sharp opposition of white-collar and professional unions. The white-collar unions agreed to a five-year contract which runs past the deadline of the LO agreement, thus excluding any parallelism for the time being. The problem may be difficult to solve, since all sides insist on the government staying out of bargaining.

There are no restrictions on the political activities of unions. Indeed, local union organizations may decide freely to join the Social Democratic Party or any other party, although in practice it is only the SP that is seriously involved. Indeed, the relationship between the LO and the SP has been very close, and some of the difficulties of the industrial relations system in 1980 may have been connected with the fact that for the first time in almost half a century the SP was excluded from the government. That in the end the non-Socialist government supported union demands is a sign of the power that labor possesses.

Spain

The death of General Franco in 1976 was followed by the gradual emergence into the open of the clandestine labor movement which had existed during the dictatorship. While the old trade unions of the Franco era (OSE) continued to exist, they were soon surpassed in importance by the formerly clandestine organizations, even though for quite a while the latter had no legal foundation. Even the employers preferred to bypass the old organizations and deal with the former underground unions.

Along with the government-sponsored unions and the clandestine organizations, factory committees had developed in the early 1960s, at first in the mines of Asturios. The Communist Party decided to support the new organizations, later to be known as workers' commissions. As Jose M. Maravall explained in "The Evolution of Industrial Conflict in Spain 1939-1975" (in *Labor Relations in Advanced Industrial Societies: Issues and Problems*, edited by Benjamin Martin and Everett M. Kassalow), since in due course—by 1967 at the latest—the non-Communists abandoned the commissions as Franco-sponsored, the Communists succeeded in dominating them. This later gave them a basis for their strong role in the labor movement.

By April 1977 an important step was taken with the enactment, by the old Franco Parliament, of the "Law to regulate the right to associate in trade unions." While the law recognized the right of workers to form unions—provided they had deposited their constitutions with a government agency—the right to strike and the freedom of assembly remained severely restricted. The ratification by the Spanish government of ILO Conventions 87 and 98 concerning freedom of association and the right to bargain collectively gradually led toward a relaxation of government regulations. Thus, after democratic elections to parliament had been held in June 1977, compulsory payment of dues to the government-sponsored unions, which were in fact part of the dictatorial regime, was abolished. In due course these organizations ceased to exist, and efforts to salvage parts of the old system were abandoned. Benjamin Martin pointed out in "Labor Relations in Post-Franco Spain: The First Four Years" (a paper submitted to the IRRA Congress in 1979) that this merely sanctioned what had already happened, as far as the trade unions were concerned. By that time, the majority of the plant delegates *(jurados de empresa)*, the official workers' representatives, had been elected on lists proposed by the anti-Franco organizations. But progress beyond this point proved painfully slow. In the absence of legal developments, the now-legal trade unions operated freely.

Two main labor organizations emerged: the Workers' Commissions Confederation (WC), linked with the Communist Party, and the General Union of Workers (UGT), cooperating with the Socialist Workers Party. Because of the close relations with political parties, the main decisions in the area of industrial relations were made in the political arena. The decisive event was the outcome of the parliamentary elections in June 1977 which gave the Socialists almost as many votes as the government party (UCD) and almost three times as many votes as the Communists. Yet while the UGT thereby received a strong boost, the WC managed to elect 34 percent of the workers' delegates in 1978, while the UGT lagged behind with 22 percent. In view of the weakness of the new democratic regime and of unfavorable economic developments, the unions accepted a somewhat passive role which in turn weakened the unions themselves. At the same time the parties of the left committed themselves to a political truce. In the elections of March 1979 this resulted in a sharp setback for the Socialists to the benefit of the UCD and Prime Minister Suarez. Since the Socialist threat to its power was diminished, the government was now more ready to make concessions to the unions and to abandon its earlier barely concealed preference for the Communists as allies against the Socialists.

Employers and the UGT joined in an effort to obtain a labor code that would greatly reduce government control of industrial relations as well as Communist labor hegemony. A labor statute was then enacted which will make possible the growth of free collective bargaining. While Martin described the new legislation as "somewhat partial to employer interests," it permits at long last the growth of an industrial relations system in line with those in force in most democratic countries of Western Europe, and it guarantees the essential freedoms of trade unionism.

Conclusion

In their early days trade unions were confronted by the resistance of employers and, frequently, the authorities. Employers opposed unions as restrictions on the right to property; public authorities perceived unions as potential sources of rebellion and threats to the existing order of things. Gradually over the second half of the nineteenth century these attitudes changed, though the changes were often accompanied by violent strife.

Beginning in this century and varying from country to country, most employers came to accept unions and collective bargaining. The extension of collective bargaining into areas not directly concerned with wages, working conditions, and fringe benefits is still looked on by many managements as illegitimate. Nevertheless, business executives are slowly accepting, though often reluctantly, new developments in industrial relations.

As to governments, their early repressive attitude has given way to support or at least acceptance of trade unions in all democratic countries. Indeed, government attitudes toward unions can be used as a touchstone to ascertain the degree to which they respond to the needs and wishes of the great mass of citizens.

It is fair to say that there is now no democratic government in any industrial country of the West which wishes to destroy or dominate the unions. At times there are conflicts and disagreements over policies and trade union tactics, but there are no more attempts to undermine or control the labor organizations. No longer are the unions regarded as subversive or as intolerable interferences with the freedom of the market. Indeed, in a number of countries, especially after World War I, policies to *encourage* unionism and collective bargaining were enacted. At the same time, in most democratic countries, the International Labor Organization pointed out (in *Collective Bargaining in Industrialized Market Economies*), public authorities "conceived their role in collective bargaining to be a limited one, centered on the maintenance of industrial peace, the facilitation of industrial bargaining machinery, and the protection of workers in their exercise of their freedom of association."

As Johannes Schregle wrote in the ILO's "Industrial Relations in the Public Sector" (in *The Changing Patterns of Industrial Relations in Asian Countries*), even for the public sector there is a "general principle, widely accepted that employees...have the same right as workers in the private sector to establish and join organizations of their own choosing without previous authorization, and to enjoy adequate protection in the exercise of this right against interference from the government or, as the case may be, the employer. The Freedom of Association and Protection of the Right to Organize Convention, 1948 (No. 87) of the ILO, applies equally to the private and public sectors with the sole exception of the armed forces and the police....This Convention protects the right to organize from undue interference by the government.

"The Right to Organize and Collective Bargaining Convention, 1949 (No. 98), which is mainly aimed at protecting workers against employers' acts of anti-union victimization...applies to both the public and private sectors, but its Article 6 excepts from its scope public servants engaged in the administration of the state." The main problems in industrial relations in the public sector pertain to the reaction of management rather than to the policies of the unions. It is an indication of the spirit of free nations how they solve this problem. The issue is how to combine the maximum of flexibility for the management of the public enterprise with the ultimate responsibility, especially for public finances, and other policies of the government. A variety of solutions or compromises have been developed, but the tendency has been toward growing freedom of unionism and collective bargaining. Closely linked with this problem is that of the right to strike. However, the crucial factor is not the nature of the ownership of the enterprise, but rather the government's duty to maintain public health, order, and security. Even where public opinion finds it difficult to distinguish between the two factors—ownership and the nature of the activity—the principle underlying this distinction is gradually coming to be accepted. Moreover, the ILO's Schregle has pointed out that "it is...necessary that in every case in which certain workers are prohibited from striking, adequate guarantees should be accorded to such workers in order fully to guarantee their interests."

True, in the U.S. elaborate legislation as well as the supervision of regulatory agencies affects union organizational work as well as their collective bargaining activities. But practically all of this governmental or semi-governmental intervention relates to procedural rather than substantive issues. On the other hand, the attempt of the British Conservative government to follow the U.S. example, with some variations, by way of the Industrial Relations Act of 1971 failed, and even the procedural aspects of industrial relations in the U.K. are left to the self-regulation of the unions. Thus, observed Otto Kahn-Freund in "Report on the Legal Status of Collective Bargaining and Collective Agreements in Great Britain" (in *Labour Relations and the Law*), it continues to be true at least for the time being that "in a country in which collective bargaining is so highly developed and of such comparatively ancient origin, the bulk of collective bargaining and collective agreements continues to exist outside the law and without any development of a 'collective labor law' of any major proportions."

In varying degrees this desire to avoid state intervention in industrial relations—apart from extreme emergencies such as war, major economic disturbances, especially the threat of inflation—has led the national organizations of employers as well as employees in several industrial countries to develop their own procedural arrangements, particularly as regards the settlement of industrial disputes. Among these countries are the U.S., the U.K., Germany, Sweden, and Switzerland. The main issue standing in the way of further developments along these voluntaristic lines is the possibility that inflation will provoke governments to impose income policies or direct supervision of wages and prices, if only temporarily, for the duration of the inflationary crisis.

A peculiar kind of distinction has developed between two different kinds of countries: the U.S., on the one hand, stressing the regulation of procedures, has a minimum of substantive laws and rules in the industrial relations area; most of the continental countries, on the other hand, leave procedural matters to the bargaining partners but have more elaborate laws as to minimum standards of pay, working conditions, and so forth. Great Britain, having made an unsuccessful attempt to join the U.S. in its approach, falls outside the two groups, with practically no government-imposed procedural rules and few substantive minimum standards. Although these statements oversimplify matters, they contain enough truth to offer insights into the fundamentals of the various sytems. An explanation suggested in the ILO's *Collective Bargaining in Industrialized Market Economies* points out that industry-wide agreements, of necessity neglecting many details, offer fewer occasions for procedural disputes than the enterprise or even plant agreements common in the U.S. But the purpose of most labor regulations in practically all industrial countries of the West since the end of World War II has been to assist unions rather than obstruct them. Bringing some measure of order to often historically determined organizational chaos may damage particular interests; this is probably unavoidable regardless of whether the initiative comes from the state or the trade union confederation.

Thus a new balance of relationships between unions, management, and the government is likely to emerge in the course of the next few years. What matters is less the detail of this relationship than the preservation of basic freedoms: the existence of free, independent trade unions responsible to their members for the defense of their interests; and the maintenance of free governments, elected by and responsible to their citizens, and emerging out of free competitive elections.

Workers' Rights in the Soviet Union and Eastern Europe

By Adrian Karatnycky and Alexander J. Motyl

Soviet Union

INTRODUCTION

Soviet trade unions are organized along branch lines paralleling Soviet ministries. There are thirty such divisions, ranging from agriculture and procurements to education to higher schools and scientific institutions to geology to trade and consumer cooperatives. Under this structure both rank-and-file workers and their managers are represented by the same union, even though their interests may differ or conflict.

As a result of this structure, writes Professor Jerry Hough in *How the Soviet Union Is Governed*, "there is a close relationship between the branch trade unions and the ministries. Indeed, since administrators as well as workers . . . are trade union members, top ministerial officials can be elected to the central committees of the respective trade unions."

In 1978 the combined membership of the All-Union Central Council of Trade Unions (AUCCTU) numbered 121 million workers. This number included every employed person in the Soviet Union with the exception of those working for the military or the police.

While the constituent trade unions are established along branch lines, the Central Council of Trade Unions is organized according to functions. The interrelationship of the Council of Trade Unions and the government is clearly demonstrated by the fact that the Council frequently issues joint decrees with government ministries. These decrees affect work time, vacations, wages, and working conditions. In addition, joint appeals by the Council of Trade Unions and the Central Committee of the Communist Party of the Soviet Union (CPSU) are also issued.

According to Western experts on Soviet politics, the relative power of trade union leaders is not very high. A regional trade union leader is estimated to rank no higher than eleventh among civilian officials. Low priority is likewise attached to the position of chairman of the AUCCTU, and is attested to by the fact that from May 1975 to November 1976, the position was left vacant.

In theory trade unions in the U.S.S.R. are entitled to participate in drafting economic plans and labor legislation. They are likewise entitled to play a role in influencing the determination of wages, work norms, and safety measures. Yet according to Valery Chalidze, an exiled human rights activist and an expert on Soviet labor law, "the existing government-controlled trade unions in the U.S.S.R. [are] in practice a branch of the administration and not representative of workers in the conflict with management." In the view of another expert on the Soviet working class, Vadim Belotserkovsky, a former industrial correspondent in the U.S.S.R. who now lives in West Germany, the function of trade unions consists of "organizing labor resources, trying to increase labor productivity, and exercising control over the labor force." In reality, he concludes, they are an arm of the state.

THE RIGHT TO FORM TRADE UNIONS

Article 95 of the Fundamentals of Labor Legislation of the U.S.S.R. and the Union Republics (which became effective January 1, 1980) states:

> In keeping with the Constitution of the U.S.S.R., factory and office workers shall be guaranteed freedom of association in trade unions. Trade unions shall function in conformity with the rules they adopt and shall not be required to register with state bodies.

The 1977 Soviet Constitution also implies the right to create independent trade unions: "In accordance with the goals of communist construction, citizens of the U.S.S.R. have the right to unite in public organizations that facilitate the development of political activity and initiative, and the satisfaction of their diverse interests." Yet it should be kept in mind that the phrase *in accordance with the goals of communist construction* can be interpreted to restrict the manner in which the right to form trade unions can be exercised.

Indeed, under Article 6 of the Soviet Constitution, the Communist Party is defined to be the "leading and guiding force of Soviet society and the nucleus of its political system and of all state and public organizations." Consequently, the full independence of trade unions appears to be circumscribed by this declaration and violates the international obligations to which the U.S.S.R. is bound as a signatory of the International Labor Organization (ILO) Convention 87, Article 3 of which guarantees the full right of organizing activities and formulating programs to all workers' organizations.

Thus, a 1979 report by the Committee of Experts on the Application of Conventions and Recommendations of the ILO concluded:

> The term *public organizations,* used in [the provision of the 1977 Soviet Constitution cited above] seems to cover workers' organizations. If so, the committee can only observe that the law (in this case the Constitution of the state) establishes a link between the Communist Party and the workers' organizations in which the leading role falls as of right and permanently to the party. Thus, even, if the policy of this party is carried out through workers' organizations in accordance with procedures laid down in their rules, the legal system does not seem to accord these organizations the full right to organize the activities and formulate their programs as provided by Article 3 of the Convention.

Even better indicators of the extent to which the right to form trade unions is guaranteed in the Soviet Union are the Soviet government's responses to attempts made since 1977 to establish trade unions free from government control.

In November 1977 a group of workers and unemployed led by a former coalminer from the Donbas region of the Ukraine, Vladimir Klebanov, announced the formation of the Association of Free Trade Unions of Workers in the Soviet Union (AFTU). In an appeal to Western trade unions and the International Labor Organization, AFTU stated:

> On the one hand, the party and government call upon citizens to correct violations wherever they occur...On the other hand, the authorities come down with special brutality on those...who [speak] out in the interests of the enterprise. All our attempts to obtain justice from the authorities have been in vain.

That the Klebanov group was a legitimate trade union organization is unquestionable, as a look at their Charter reveals. That document states:

> The purposes of the Association of Free Trade Unions are: a. to carry out the obligations reached by collective bargaining; b. to induce workers and other employees to join free trade union associations; c. to carry out those decisions of the Association which concern the defense of rights and the seeking of justice; d. to educate Association members in the spirit of irreconcilability toward deficiencies, bureaucracy, deception, inefficiency and wastefulness, and a negligent attitude toward national wealth.

These purposes, as well as the Charter's principle of including in its ranks "any worker or employee whose rights and interests have been unlawfully violated by administrative, governmental, party, or judicial agencies," indicate that AFTU was in every sense an organization whose right to exist is guaranteed by the U.S.S.R.'s international obligations.

Yet the repression of AFTU activists was swift and sure. Vladimir Klebanov was arrested by the Soviet police on December 19, 1977, along with two other workers in Donetsk. Nine days later, after international protests against his confinement, Klebanov was released. Worker Gavriil Yankov was confined for two weeks in a Moscow psychiatric hospital, and AFTU members Tsvyrko and Reznichenko were imprisoned by Soviet authorities. On February 1, 1978, AFTU publicly announced the establishment of its organizational Charter. Several days later Association members Guryev, Kucherenko, Poplavsky, and Luchkov were detained by Soviet authorities on charges of not having official permission to reside in Moscow. Vladimir Klebanov was again seized by Soviet police and transferred from Moscow to a psychiatric prison hospital in Donestk, in the Ukrainian S.S.R. Group member Nikolaev was also seized and placed under psychiatric detention, as were workers Dvoretsky and Pelekh. Vladimir Klebanov remains imprisoned in a psychiatric hospital to this day.

The pattern to the repression of AFTU activists is all too apparent. To have arrested them on political charges (i.e., "slander against the state" or "anti-Soviet agitation and propaganda") would have been to admit that there is worker discontent in the U.S.S.R. From the point of view of Soviet propaganda considerations it was much better to imprison AFTU activists in psychiatric hospitals and argue that their discontent was the product of insanity.

By October 1978 it was clear that repressions and arrests had resulted in the breaking up of AFTU. But the cause of trade union rights was to be raised by a new group, the Free Interprofessional Association of Workers (known by its Russian acronym, SMOT). SMOT held its first press conference in Moscow on October 28, 1978. A leading figure in the leadership of SMOT was electrician Vladimir Borisov. Borisov, a native of Leningrad, had been interned in Soviet psychiatric hospitals for a total of nine years in the 1960s and 1970s for his human rights activities and, unlike

Klebanov, had close links to the human rights movement in the U.S.S.R.

Having learned from the experience of the Klebanov-led AFTU, SMOT decided not to reveal publicly the names of all its members. At the time of its formation SMOT was comprised of eight autonomous groups, representing approximately one hundred members. According to the organization's Western representative, Victor Fainberg, by June 1979 SMOT numbered ten autonomous groups with a total membership of two hundred.

SMOT functions on the following basis: Each autonomous constituent group elects one representative to serve on a council, whose decisions have the force of recommendations. In addition, SMOT has established a Working Commission for the Defense of Economic, Social, Religious, and Political Rights of Workers in the U.S.S.R. This commission publishes an information bulletin which reports on searches, arrests, detentions, and harassment of workers and independent trade union activists in the U.S.S.R.

As in the case of AFTU, SMOT's founding document indicates that the organization's goals are fully consonant with the goals of an independent trade union organization. Among SMOT's purposes are:

> the defense of its members in cases of the violation of their rights in various spheres of their daily activities: economic, social, cultural, spiritual, religious, domestic, and political. This defense is to be carried out by all possible means within the framework of the Constitution and international agreements signed by the Soviet government. Furthermore, SMOT intends to look into the legal bases of the complaints of workers; to ensure that these complaints are brought to the notice of relevant organizations; to facilitate a quick solution to workers' complaints; and in cases of negative results, to publicize them widely before the Soviet and international public. In order to give stronger assistance to workers who are not members of SMOT, a working commission is also being organized.

Yet despite the evidence that SMOT's activity was not in any sense illegal, Soviet authorities began their repression of SMOT activists even before the group had held its first public meeting. Fifteen days before the SMOT press conference, Vladimir Skvirsky, a 48-year-old geologist and member of the Council of Representatives of SMOT, was arrested and placed in a Moscow prison for investigation. He was charged with "theft of state property" under Article 94, paragraph 1, of the Criminal Code of the Russian Soviet Federated Socialist Republic (R.S.F.S.R.), which provides for up to three years' imprisonment in forced labor camps upon conviction. Skvirsky's alleged crime consisted of a failure to pay fines for damaged library books. During his trial in May 1979 Skvirsky insisted that he had indeed paid fines totalling the full value of the damaged books, pleaded not guilty, and during the investigation period of his detention, refused to answer all questions concerning his activities in SMOT. Despite the fact that Skvirsky's complete innocence had been proven, he was sentenced to five years' internal exile.

In December 1978 Mark Morozov, a computer engineer who had agreed to join SMOT, was also incarcerated, on charges of anti-Soviet agitation. In November and December 1978, the homes of SMOT activists were searched by Soviet police, and SMOT members Borisov, Lev Volokhonsky, Albina Yakoreva, and Valeriya Novodvorskaya were arrested and detained by Soviet authorities. Both Novodvorskaya and Borisov have been held in psychiatric hospitals.

On March 20, 1979, Lev Volokhonsky, a 34-year-old worker and member of the SMOT Council of Representatives, was incarcerated in Moscow's Lefortovo prison. He was charged with "distribution of libelous allegations known to be false and defaming the Soviet state and public regime" (Article 190, paragraph 1, of the Criminal Code of the R.S.F.S.R.). On June 12, 1979, Volokhonsky was sentenced to two years' forced labor.

Throughout 1979 and 1980 SMOT activists have been subjected to extra-judicial persecution, harassment, and threats. In January 1980 SMOT member Yuri Grimm was arrested by Soviet authorities and incarcerated in Moscow's Butyrka prison. He is currently imprisoned while awaiting the conclusion of the investigation of his case—a common Soviet practice. On March 27, 1980, Vladimir Borisov was arrested and incarcerated in Leningrad Psychiatric Hospital Number 3. Following protests by American and West European trade unions, Soviet authorities released Borisov on May 3, 1980. In June 1980 Borisov was forcibly expelled from the Soviet Union.

The pattern of repression against the AFTU and SMOT groups demonstrates that the right to form trade unions in the U.S.S.R. is so severely impeded by Soviet authorities that it can be safely asserted that this right is nonexistent.

THE DEFENSE OF WORKERS' RIGHTS BY OFFICIAL TRADE UNIONS

The Fundamentals of Labor Legislation of the U.S.S.R. and the Union Republics indicates that it is the duty of trade unions to actively defend the interests of working people. Yet the preamble to the bylaws of Soviet trade unions indicates quite clearly what the "central task" of these organizations is:

> The central task of the trade unions is to mobilize the masses for the attainment of our principal economic goal—the creation of the material and technical basis of communism, for the further strengthening of the Soviet Union's economic and defense power, for ensuring a steady rise in the people's material and cultural standards.
>
> The Soviet trade unions direct their activities toward securing a further and powerful advance in all branches of the economy, fulfillment and overfulfillment of economic plans, promotion of technical progress and an uninterrupted rise in labor productivity, and in the effectiveness of social production, toward the lowering of labor input, rational utilization and economy of raw materials and material resources, improvement of the quality of the products, better use of the production funds and of investment capital. Trade unions jointly with the organs of management organize socialist emulation among workers, collective farmers, engineers and technicians, and office employees, they organize the movement for a communist attitude toward work, the mass technical creativity of the toilers, they help the workers, the collective farmers and the white-collar workers to improve their productivity, their skills, and their economic and juridical knowledge, they conduct propaganda regarding production and technique, spread the experience of front-rank workers and innovators of production, promote the introduction of advanced technologies and scientific achivements in industry, agriculture, and other branches of the national economy. Trade unions direct the work of the Society of Inventors and Rationalizers and of the Science and Technology Societies.

This "central task" of Soviet trade unions of fulfilling economic plans and insuring productivity generally negates their role as a defender of the interests of workers.

The Klebanov-led AFTU and SMOT have both decried the inadequacy of official trade unions in defending the rights of workers. AFTU declared: "In our country there is no institution that objectively defends our rights. Soviet trade unions do not defend our rights and do not have the necessary authority." SMOT has stated: "In our country today there is no organization independent of the state authorities which could directly represent the workers."

As Valery Chalidze has written, "What is the principal weakness of the Soviet workers' legal position? It is not the lack of statutes regulating hours, safety measures, etc., since such statutes exist. The guarantees may be imperfect, but many problems would be solved if the regulations were enforced. It is not local management's failure to observe the labor regulations and its tendency to drive the workers in an effort to fulfill the plan, since such conflicts between management and workers are predictable and occur in other countries as well. The main problem is that workers lack any possibility for conducting a legal struggle in defense of their rights.... The existing trade unions are controlled by the authorities and strive for fulfillment of the plan and strengthening of labor discipline; they do not make a serious effort to safeguard the workers' rights."

In the final analysis, one of the most telling indictments against the official trade unions in the U.S.S.R. is that in not a single instance have they undertaken to defend workers who have been imprisoned or incarcerated in psychiatric hospitals for their activities in SMOT or AFTU.

THE RIGHT TO STRIKE

Nowhere in Soviet law is the right to strike expressly permitted. It might therefore be argued that the right to strike is not expressly forbidden. Yet Article 190 of the Criminal Code of the R.S.F.S.R. (and parallel articles in the criminal codes of the other republics), contains a statute which can be applied against striking workers. It states:

> Organization of, as well as active participation in, group actions grossly infringing public order or entailing manifest disobedience to legal orders of the representatives of power or having resulted in disturbance of the work of transport [or] of state [or] social institutions or enterprises—is punished by deprivation of liberty for up to three years, or by corrective labor for up to one year, or by a fine of up to 100 rubles.

Moreover, Soviet practice in dealing with strikes is unequivocal. In 1969, for example, a factory-wide strike in a Chervonograd electrical plant resulted in the firing of the strike's instigators within three months of the work stoppage. The strike leader was imprisoned for one year on charges of theft, although he had been employed at the factory for twenty-four years. Another strike in 1969 at the Kiev hydroelectric station in the Ukrainian S.S.R. resulted in the arrest of strike leader Ivan Hryshchuk. According to former political prisoner Leonid Plyushch, Hryshchuk is to this day incarcerated in Dnipropetrovsk Special Psychiatric Hospital.

A 1971 strike at the Kirov factory in Kopeyske was put down by Soviet authorities, and the KGB was reported to have arrested the organizers of the strike at what is the largest equipment factory in the U.S.S.R.

In December 1972 a strike in Kamenets-Podolsk, in the Ukraine, demanded a lowering of output quotas. Thirty workers, each with more than twenty years employment at the factory, were dismissed for being instigators of the strike. Two of them were sentenced to three years' deprivation of freedom.

These examples confirm Valery Chalidze's conclusion that:

> Soviet workers lack even the traditional instrument for the defense of their interests, the opportunity to strike. Soviet labor legislation does not recognize strikes as means of defending workers' rights. Organizers and participants of strikes can be charged with criminal offenses. That is the real weakness in the workers' legal position.

Furthermore, there is a fundamental hostility to strikes in Soviet ideology, which views them as phenomena which spring up in response to capitalist exploitation. Obviously they can, then, have no place in a socialist society which is in the process of constructing communism.

INTERNAL UNION DEMOCRACY

The preamble to the bylaws of Soviet trade unions states:

> The trade unions do their work under the direction of the Communist Party of the Soviet Union, which is the organizing and leading force in Soviet society.... The trade unions of the U.S.S.R. gather the workers, collective farmers, and white-collar workers

> around the party, mobilize them in the struggle for the construction of a Communist society.

That internal democracy does not exist under circumstances where the leading role of a single political party is guaranteed in the bylaws of trade unions can hardly be open to question. Indeed, all trade union activity is controlled by the party, which also monopolizes state power. Leading trade union officials are de facto chosen by the Politburo of the Central Committee of the CPSU. Illustrative of this state of affairs is the case of Alexander Shelepin. In May 1975 Shelepin was dismissed from his position in the Politburo. Several days later it was announced that he had resigned from his position as trade union leader "at his own request." He was succeeded to his post by Alexei Shibaev, a former director of an aerospace enterprise, regional party secretary and Central Committee member, who had not been a member of the AUCCTU and who did not have a known record of trade union activity. In fact no reference was even made to the change in trade union leadership at a subsequent congress of the AUCCTU.

Indicative of the subordinate role of trade unions as an institution controlled by the party, and of the absence of internal union democracy, was Leonid Brezhnev's 1977 speech to the Congress of the AUCCTU. In the middle of his presentation Brezhnev referred to a discussion that was proceeding on the need to reform trade unions. The first secretary defended the necessity for reform by arguing that it would improve the structure and efficiency of trade unions. Yet no one at the Congress inquired about the discussion of reform. No one asked who was involved in this discussion; no one inquired where it was taking place or what points the discussion had raised.

According to Vadim Belotserkovsky, who for many years was a reporter with *Izvestiya*, a daily Soviet newspaper:

> such discussion takes place within the ruling party. The party decides the policy, the activities, and the personnel of the unions. At the lowest levels union officials do go through the formality of an election, but there is only one candidate, chosen by the relevant party organization. And above the middle ranks of the unions, even such formal election procedures are dispensed with: officials are directly appointed from above by the party. The workers know very well where the power lies. They know that anyone who genuinely tried to defend the workers' interests would have to do business first with the party, then with the KGB.

ANTI-WORKER MEASURES

While a number of the undemocratic and repressive practices outlined above have a specifically anti-worker content (repression of independent trade union activists, subordination of the trade unions to party and government control, absence of internal union democracy, repression of strike leaders, etc.), Soviet workers confront a number of additional anti-worker measures. Foremost among these is the labor book. The labor book is a worker's record of employment and is often used as a means of restricting a worker's free choice of employment. In addition, the labor book can contain highly compromising information about a worker, even though the basis of such information can be an extra-judicial decision. A recent statute in Soviet labor legislation provides that: "an entry shall be made in the labor book of a person performing corrective labor without deprivation of liberty to the effect that the period of corrective labor is not to be reckoned toward the total length of uninterrupted employment" (Article 15). From a civil liberties point of view, this practice allows management to have access to personal information about sanctions which were taken against a worker outside the court system. Once entered into a labor book, such a "blemish" on a worker's record can follow him for the rest of his life.

Furthermore, trade unions themselves impose disciplinary measures against workers who fail to fulfill their duties, which according to union regulations include: raising labor productivity, contributing to the defense power of the U.S.S.R., observing state and labor discipline, and combatting antisocial conduct.

Management can impose disciplinary measures for breach of labor discipline in the form of "reproof," "reprimand," "severe reprimand," "transfer to a lower-paying post for no more than three months," or "dismissal." However, breach of labor discipline can also be punished through the mechanism of trade union run "comrades' courts." These extra-judiciary bodies can impose punishments ranging from public apology and comradely warning to public social condemnation and recommendation that management apply the punishment of demotion to a lower-paid post or demotion to a lower grade of work.

A most pernicious anti-worker institution is the so-called *pervoi otdel*, the "first section." The first section is in effect the personnel department of a given factory or enterprise, which has direct links to the KGB. Thus it is a mechanism for screening out ideologically undesirable employees or workers who have participated in dissident activities without having broken any laws.

CONCLUSION

As this study has attempted to demonstrate, in all areas of trade union rights Soviet performance is inconsistent with democratic and human rights principles. Moreover, in the period since the signing of the Helsinki Accords, there has not only been no noticeable improvement in the rights enjoyed by workers, rather there has been severe repression of indepedent trade union activists. This repression has intensified, in particular, since 1977, the year of the formation of the Klebanov-led AFTU, and has continued virtually uninterrupted ever since.

Finally, not only has Soviet practice not been in keeping with its international human rights obligations, but according to the report of the International Labor Organization Committee of Experts on the Application of Conventions and Recommendations, the new Soviet Constitution, enacted since the signing of the Helsinki Accords "does not seem to give [trade union] organizations the full right to organize activities and formulate their programs...."

Poland

INTRODUCTION

The official trade union movement in Poland is organized in the Polish Trade Unions Federation, an umbrella organization consisting of twenty-three branch unions representing twenty-three different industries. Branch unions have from one to seventeen regional unions (represented by workers' councils at the plant level), depending on how many of Poland's seventeen administrative regions contain the industry represented by the branch union. The governing body of the Polish Trade Unions Federation is the Central Council of Trade Unions. Since membership in the Federation is compulsory, 13,067,700 workers, or about 95 percent of the working people of Poland, belonged to it as of 1977.

According to the Polish Constitution, "The Polish People's Republic is a republic of working people," so that "the power belongs to the working people of town and country" and the "laws...express the interests and the will of the working people" (Article 1, paragraph 2; Article 8, paragraph 1).

Among the many rights constitutionally guaranteed Poland's working people are the following:

• "Work is the right and the duty of, and a matter of honor for, every citizen" (Article 19, paragraph 1).

• "The Polish People's Republic guarantees its citizens freedom of speech, of the press, of meetings and assemblies, of processions and demonstrations."

• "The granting to working people and their organizations of the use of printing shops, stocks of paper, public buildings and halls, means of communication, the radio, and other indispensable material means serves to put this freedom into effect" (Article 83, paragraphs 1-2).

• "The Polish People's Republic guarantees to its citizens the right to unite in public organizations."

• "Political organizations, trade unions, and other social organizations unite the citizens for active participation in political, social, economic, and cultural life" (Article 84, paragraphs 1-2).

• "Trade unions play an important part in the Polish People's Republic, representing the interests of the working people" (Article 85).

Constitutionally, it would appear that workers and workers' rights are more than adequately protected in Poland. Yet the workers' disturbances on the Baltic Coast in 1970, in Central Poland in 1976, and the wave of strikes that swept all of Poland from Wroclaw to Warsaw to Gdansk in the summer months of 1980 just as clearly suggest that Polish workers do not perceive the "republic of the working people," whose laws purportedly express their "interests" and "will," as actually safeguarding their rights.

THE RIGHT TO FORM UNIONS

The Polish Labor Code adopted on June 26, 1974, would appear to guarantee the right of workers to form trade unions: "Workers shall have the right to associate in trade unions" (Article 19, paragraph 1). Yet other laws of the country as well as the Polish government's own practice with regard to this question directly contravene this very explicitly stated right.

As the International Confederation of Free Trade Unions (ICFTU) and the International Metalworkers Federation argued in a complaint against the government of Poland before the Committee on Freedom of Association of the International Labor Organization (ILO) on July 17, 1978, "the Polish Trade Unions Act of July 1949 contravenes the Freedom of Association and Protection of the Right to Organize, Convention 87 of 1948," which Poland voluntarily adopted. According to the ICFTU, "every new trade union [in Poland] must join the Federation by registering...; any union failing to do so (unwilling or unable to do so) would be deprived of any legal existence as a trade union."

The ICFTU concluded that "these provisions infringe the guarantees prescribed in Convention 87, according to which workers must have the right to establish organizations of their own choosing, and especially, if they so desire, a new organization independent of all other existing organizations." After judging both the ICFTU's complaint and the Polish government's reply, the ILO Committee on Freedom of Association:

> went on to refer to the constitution and rules of the Trade Unions Federation (adopted in 1954). It was provided therein that the constitution and rules of each trade union should be based on those of the Federation. Consequently, pointed out the Committee, unions wishing to become registered with the Central Council of

> Trade Unions must accept the various basic principles enunciated in the constitution and rules of the Federation, including in particular, the recognition of the guiding role of the Polish United Workers' Party. The constitution of occupational associations would appear, therefore, to be subject to certain conditions of a political nature.
>
> The Committee recalled, inter alia, that according to the provisions of Convention 87 workers, without distinction whatsoever, should have the right to establish organizations of their own choosing without previous authorization.

The Polish authorities, meanwhile, have contravened their own laws on the right of workers "to associate in trade unions" by systematically subjecting to various forms of persecution the leading worker activists of the unofficial Free Trade Unions movement, which currently consists of the Committee for Free Trade Unions (founded in Katowice on February 23, 1978), the Founding Committee of the Free Trade Unions of the Baltic Seaboard (Gdansk, April 29, 1978), and the Founding Committee of the Free Trade Unions of Western Pomerania (Szczecin, October 11, 1979). The following examples illustrate the Polish authorities' harassment of workers engaged in the free trade unions:

- In 1978 Kazimierz Switon of the Katowice Committee was detained by the police for forty-eight hours on no less than twelve occasions; jailed in August for five weeks on a trumped-up charge; and jailed for two months beginning in October for "causing a crowd to gather" while leaving church services with his family.
- Bogdan Cygan of the Katowice Committee was savagely beaten by policemen after being driven to a secluded wood beyond the city lines.
- Wladyslaw Sulecki, also of the Katowice Committee, was twice attacked by "unknown" assailants and ultimately forced to emigrate to the Federal Republic of Germany.
- Krzysztof Wyszkowski of the Gdansk Committee was arrested by the police on May 28, 1978, for his free trade union activities.

The Polish government's explanation of its action with regard to the free trade union committees and their activists is that theirs are "activities of a political nature" and that their "grievances are mainly of a political nature and so are the aims they pursue." In branding the free trade union committees as political, the Polish government has not only adopted a position opposed to that of both the ICFTU and the ILO Committee on Freedom of Association, but has also provided itself with legal justification for opposing the free trade unions. Article 81, paragraph 3, of the Polish Constitution makes clear that "The setting up of and participation in associations whose aims or activities are directed against the political and social structure or against the legal order of the Polish People's Republic are forbidden." According to this logic, since the free trade union committees are outside the Trade Unions Federation, they are "directed against the political and social structure" and, therefore, can be "forbidden."

The ILO Committee on Freedom of Association, on the other hand, has stated:

> The Committee recalls that Article 10 of Convention 87 contains a very broad definition of the term *organization*. This Article reads: "In this Convention the term *organization* means any organization of workers or of employers for furthering and defending the interests of workers or of employers."...It appears that the organization concerned [the Baltic Seaboard Trade Union Committee] pursues objectives which are included in Article 10 quoted above. Moreover, the Committee considers that a workers' organization ought to be considered as such even if it is not in a position to fulfill functions that are typically associated with trade unions, for example, collective bargaining.

Significantly, the Inter-Factory Strike Committee, formed in mid-August 1980 to represent some 250,000 striking workers from the shipyards and factories of Gdansk, Gdynia, Sopot, Elbag, Szczecin, and other cities on the Baltic coast, formally demanded of the Polish government that it accept "free trade unions independent of the Communist Party and of enterprises, in accordance with Convention 87 of the International Labor Organization concerning the right to form free trade unions, which was ratified by the Communist government of Poland."

Although in the aftermath of the August 1980 strikes the Polish government grudgingly acknowledged the right of workers to form trade unions independent of the Polish Trade Unions Federation, it is still far too early to tell whether the embryonic Gdansk-based Independent Trade Union, founded in late August 1980, will actually develop into an alternative trade union movement. The years following the worker disturbances of 1956, when the supposedly independent workers' councils created that year were eventually co-opted into the official trade union movement, may be instructive with regard to the ultimate fate of the recently formed Independent Trade Union.

THE DEFENSE OF WORKERS' RIGHTS BY OFFICIAL TRADE UNIONS

According to the Polish Labor Code, the tasks of Polish trade unions are as follows:

> The trade unions shall take part in formulating and carrying out the tasks connected with the social and economic development of the nation, the improvement of conditions of work and the workers' standard of living, and the exertion of influence on the standard of social awareness and socialist human relationships. They shall more particularly cooperate with the competent organs of government in issuing and applying the provisions of labor law and shall take action to reinforce the rule of law in connection with the observance of the workers' rights and obligations.

A conflict of aims, which manifests itself in trade union practice and evokes widespread complaints from Polish workers, is already evident in this passage: on the one hand the trade unions are to improve working conditions and workers' living standards, while on the other they are to cooperate with the government "in issuing and applying the provisions of labor law" and fostering "socialist human relationships." In other words, the trade unions represent workers *and* the state—the employees and the employer—and in this respect are subject to an inherent tension which usually goes against the interests of the workers.

The Polish Constitution reveals the source of this tension, the political subordination of trade unions to the Communist Party, in Article 3:

> The Polish United Workers' Party [PUWP] is the leading political force in the building of socialism.
>
> Cooperation among the Polish United Workers' Party, the United Peasants' Party, and the Democratic Party is the basis of the National Unity Front.
>
> The National Unity Front forms the common platform of action of the social organizations of the working people [including trade unions] and the patriotic associations of all citizens.

Moreover, as Edmund Baluka, the chairman of the strike committee in the Szczecin shipyards during the workers' riots of 1970, pointed out: "The statutes of the Polish United Workers' Party state that 'the party directs the political line of the trade unions,' and the statutes of the trade unions in turn state that 'the trade unions carry out the correct line of the PUWP in the interests of the working class and the Polish nation.' "

Nevertheless, both opponents and supporters of the official trade unions agree that they are fairly effective in providing workers with social benefits involving, as one official Polish journal put it, "the supervision of labor conditions, administration of the workers' holiday fund, distribution of beds in sanatoriums, allocation of flats in houses administered by the factory, organization of workers' gardening allotments," and so forth.

While agreeing with the above sentiments, Jan Litynski, worker activist and editor of *Robotnik*, an unofficial workers' journal, claims that "for the workers, the union is just one body among others at the service of management; it concerns itself with social questions in the factory... but absolutely not with defending their interests," because "the official unions take the side of management" and their officials are "paid functionaries at the disposal of management."

Not surprisingly, one of the demands made by the Inter-Factory Strike Committee in August 1980 was the "abolition of administrative interference in trade union matters."

The situations in which official trade unions side with the authorities generally involve two sets of questions: (1) those in which management, in order to fulfill or overfulfill its production plans and quotas, will try to economize on workers' wages, extend working hours, demand productivity increases, and/or disregard costly health and safety regulations; (2) those in which workers engage in dissident or semi-dissident activities and are, as a result, dismissed from work, harassed, or subjected to other forms of reprisal.

In the first instance, the official trade unions tend to act as the transmission belts and executive arms of the party and management. Wladyslaw Sulecki, formerly of the Katowice Committee for Free Trade Unions, has provided a number of typical examples of union acquiescence in questionable management practices. For example, according to Sulecki: "The party trade union does not defend aggrieved miners. In my section [of the mine] there were instances of work assignments being fulfilled by 124 percent while the management reckoned only 90 percent. Complaints [with the union] did not help." Also: "The unions which serve the government do not care about the rights of workers. When the main cable [in the mine] was seriously damaged and the whole mine came to a standstill, the second and third shifts were cancelled. But the miners who did not come to work got reductions in pay." Again, the official trade unions did not intervene on their behalf for the sake of fulfilling the plan.

With regard to official trade union attitudes toward worker activists who step outside the bounds of officially tolerated forms of worker expression, it is sufficient to recall official trade union inactivity in the face of police harassment of the free trade union activists (see above) and persecution of the workers who engaged in the 1976 strikes. While hundreds of strikers lost their jobs and many others were incarcerated, the official unions remained silent.

Perhaps the most persuasive proof of the fact that official Polish trade unions do not adequately defend essential workers' rights is the existence of the free trade union committees mentioned above, the Workers' Defense Committee, KOR (founded on September 25, 1976, by fourteen Polish intellectuals), the Social Self-Defense Committee, KSS-KOR (an expanded version of KOR, founded in the summer of 1977), and the unofficial workers' journal *Robotnik*—all of which attempt, at the risk of serious reprisals, to defend those workers' rights which the official unions do not.

In its above-mentioned complaint, the ICFTU concluded that "it is clear... that the defense of the workers' interests is no longer assured by the official trade unions, which are imposed upon the workers since only unions registered with the Central Council of Trade Unions are allowed legally to exist."

THE RIGHT TO STRIKE

Neither the Polish Constitution nor the Polish Labor Code contains any reference to the legality or illegality of strikes. However, Article 52 of the Labor Code effectively prohibits strikes by implicitly defining them as "serious violations" of a worker's "obligations" for which he may be fired without notice.

(A worker's primary "obligations," according to the Code, are "to carry out his work conscientiously and carefully, observe labor discipline, and comply with the instructions given to him in connection with this work.") Thus, according to Article 52:

> An establishment may terminate a contract of employment without further notice through the worker's fault if (1) the worker commits a serious violation of his basic obligations as a worker, and more particularly, if he disturbs the order and peace of the workplace, is absent from his work without a valid reason.... (3) the worker commits an offense during the currency of his contract of employment that renders his further employment at his post impossible.

In practice, Article 52 of the Labor Code has indeed been used to punish striking workers. As the unofficial Charter of Workers' Rights, circulated in the summer of 1979 by the editors of *Robotnik* and other worker activists, states, "it is necessary to amend Article 52, which is utilized as an anti-strike statute...; the right to strike must be legally guaranteed."

Nevertheless, although Polish law implicitly condemns strikes and the Polish authorities explicitly oppose them, strikes do take place in Poland, and a number of them have apparently gone unpunished, at least in the immediate aftermath. In fact, in the most recent worker disturbances to have shaken Poland, hundreds of strikes—staged by factory and shipyard workers as well as bus drivers, miners, and sanitation workers—have occurred in the months of July and August 1980 alone.

Polish worker dissidents, aware of the relative effectiveness of strikes, call on workers to employ this weapon more often. According to the Charter of Workers' Rights:

> Undoubtedly, the most effective course of action is strikes, even those on a small scale. In general, these are effective merely in the short run....If the workers are able to act in solidarity and are unafraid, it is possible to force management into making concessions by the very threat of a strike: through presenting petitions or sending delegations.

However, as the Social Self-Defense Committee, KOR, underlines: "strikes last for a short time and end with short-term success. The management refunds lost wages, restores former productivity norms, or reintroduces a work-free Saturday. For the most part, however, these concessions apply to individual cases only and take a form that does not satisfy the workers." What appears to be an exception to this rule is the strike wave of August 1980, which ultimately produced government concessions on almost all of the Inter-Factory Strike Committee's demands, including the granting of the right to strike. Whether these gains will prove to be permanent is another matter. The right to strike, for example, was also granted in 1956 but was eventually rescinded in the years that followed.

The first known case of the authorities' taking no immediate action against striking workers was at the Pabianice electric bulb factory, where some 3,000 workers struck twice in August 1977 over what they believed were unjustified reductions in pay. Eventually, after the intercession of a member of the PUWP Central Committee, the workers were restored their original pay. Likewise, the Polish government's immediate reaction to the mid-1980 strikes has been conciliatory.

Other strikes, at least temporarily left unpunished by the authorities, have also reportedly occurred. But, as the Social Self-Defense Committee, KOR, pointed out: "Often, some time after the tense atmosphere [of a strike] is relieved, reprisals come for the active participants in the strikes—they are dismissed from work or transferred to worse jobs."

INTERNAL UNION DEMOCRACY

According to an official English-language Polish journal, internal trade union democracy functions in the following manner:

> The factory cell is the basic organizational unit of the trade unions in Poland. It is governed by the workers' council, elected by direct and secret ballot for a three-year term.
>
> The organization of the Polish trade unions is based on democratic centralism. This practically means that: all trade union authorities are elective; members of trade union authorities can be recalled at every request by the electors, providing their activity is inconsistent with the statute or resolutions, or they infringe the principles of social intercourse; resolutions of all trade union organizations and authorities are adopted by a majority of votes in the presence of at least a half of the membership of a given body.

Polish worker dissidents also admit that workers can—

sometimes even effectively—voice their grievances and demands in and through the official trade unions. According to the Charter of Workers' Rights:

> There are many problems at the workplace which can be resolved by making use of official trade unions. Certainly it would be better for us if these were not as inert as they usually are. It is necessary to demand that trade unions defend the interests of workers by utilizing trade union meetings for discussions, by pressing demands, by electing to the trade union leaders who will implement such demands.

Yet the scope of internal trade union democracy is severely circumscribed by two limitations. First, the trade union apparatus is dominated by PUWP members, whose primary allegiance is to the party and state. In this manner official trade unions practically become the transmission belts of party-to-worker directives.

What is more, there is reason to believe that it is the less outspoken, less independent-minded, and more pliant workers who seek positions in the trade union apparatus. As Jan Litynski, editor of *Robotnik*, has remarked: "We can see that the most active and socially committed workers go to the party rather than the unions. Why? Because the party is more powerful and has a greater presence in the workplace. The union is just a docile tool. But in the party things happen...."

Second, internal union democracy is further circumscribed, while party control is reinforced, by the fact that only 15 percent of the nominations of candidates for union positions at the factory level can be made from the floor, thereby assuring the party-dominated apparatus effective control over the choice of the union's functionaries.

Although the Polish government recently conceded to the Inter-Factory Strike Committee the right of workers to vote for an unlimited number of candidates for trade union positions by means of a secret ballot, Wladyslaw Sulecki, formerly of the Katowice Committee for Free Trade Unions, has pointed out (in another context) the inherent structural dangers that can threaten this formal right: "Should the workers choose sensitive persons who care for the working man to the workers' councils, then shortly thereafter, the Communist administration exerts pressure on these persons, remakes them as it sees fit, or simply ejects them from their positions."

In line with Sulecki's complaint, the Charter of Workers' Rights demands that union officials elected by the workforce must "be legally protected from dismissal for a certain period...."

Although the net effect of all these measures is to reduce greatly the degree and scope of internal trade union democracy, it is possible, in extraordinary situations involving atypical worker activism—as in the months following the violent workers' strikes on the Baltic coast in 1971—to exert a substantial, if only temporary, amount of influence both on the choice of the union's functionaries and on the direction of the union's policies. With the consolidation of state and party power, however, these gains are usually reversed by means of selective repression against worker leaders, job transfers, temporary acquiescence in some demands, increased bonuses, and so forth.

Ultimately, the greatest impediment to internal union democracy is that the unions, being subordinate to the Communist Party, are effectively forbidden from or incapable of broaching a wide range of worker-related issues. When questions that conflict with the party's directives—such as wage increases, changes in production quotas, or strikes—do indeed arise, internal union democracy becomes severely constricted. In other, less controversial areas dealing with social benefits, vacations, and the like, the official trade unions are far more capable vehicles for hearing and voicing worker demands.

ANTI-WORKER MEASURES

Three sets of anti-worker measures can be discerned in Poland. First, those affecting the unemployed worker; second, those relating to worker dissidents; and third, those dealing with working conditions.

Since, according to the official ideology, there neither can be nor is any unemployment in a socialist state such as Poland, there neither are nor can be, correspondingly, any unemployment benefits for workers who lose their jobs. While most unemployed workers remain so temporarily and therefore do not suffer unduly, those workers who have lost their jobs for violating the unwritten "political" code of conduct can, by means of blacklists, be kept unemployed and without an income for indefinite periods of time.

Second, worker activists who refuse to follow the party, trade union, or management line will often be harassed by means of various on- and off-the-job measures. Wladyslaw Sulecki describes his own experiences as an activist of the Social Self-Defense Committee, KOR:

> For having ties to the KSS-KOR, I, a veteran miner, was transferred to an auxiliary position. I had to work in water up to my knees, alone. I earned almost three times less than my colleagues.... The same happened to other miners and workers who sided with the KSS-KOR and supported the free trade unions. They searched their lockers. They poured glue into their locks. They harassed them in every manner. They did not give me the apartment a miner deserves... I lived in a perpetually damp room and kitchen with my wife and three daughters. When I went to the mine workers' council and said that I deserved a better apartment as a hardworking miner, I was told: "With your views you should live in barracks."

Finally, all workers—whether active dissidents or not—are often subjected to illegal or, if technically legal, clearly oppressive working conditions. As mentioned above, plant management, abetted by the official trade union, will often try to save on worker-related expenses—such as wages, bonuses, and safety measures—to the detriment of the workers.

The Charter of Workers' Rights, in its demands for changes in labor conditions, points to what it is that worker dissidents consider "anti-worker" in current Polish labor practice:

> Slowdowns, changes of norms, etc., cannot lead to the lowering of earnings.
>
> It is impermissible to be forced to work overtime or to do supplementary and voluntary work; miners must be guaranteed days off on Sundays and holidays.
>
> Rules and norms concerning work safety must be *scrupulously enforced;* ...commissions controlled by the BHP (Health and Safety Code), commissions investigating accidents, and also doctors should be *institutionally independent* of the factory administration.
>
> No one who loses his health as a result of harmful work conditions should be without his due compensation or pension.

In short, states the Charter: "the fundamental rights of working people, such as the right to safe and rational work, equitable pay, and the right to time off have been limited."

CONCLUSION

The evidence of international labor organizations to which Poland subscribes and of Polish workers themselves provides convincing proof that the five categories of workers' rights analyzed above are either legally circumscribed or practically forbidden in the People's Republic of Poland. Polish workers, however, more than any of their colleagues in the Eastern bloc countries, have revealed and continue to reveal a great deal of vitality and determination in their struggle for these rights. In spite of substantial harassment by the authorities, Polish workers are continually adapting to the evolving circumstances in their country, developing ever-new forms for advancing their interests, and proving in the process that they possess a very high degree of political awareness, as the 1980 strike wave clearly demonstrated. At present, an uneasy balance appears to have set in between the regime and the workers, with both sides mindful of each other's strengths and weaknesses and unwilling to go too far to upset the existing balance. Given such a dynamic situation, although the regime is unlikely to make concessions on fundamental rights for fear of undermining itself and antagonizing the Soviet Union, it may be willing to tolerate, as it already does, a sizable measure of worker dissent as a safety valve for growing worker discontent. Should this trend continue and worker dissent become a permanent feature of Polish society, its influence on the long-term course and nature of that society could be profound.

Rumania

INTRODUCTION

Rumanian trade unions are organized according to the field of production rather than to that of craft or trade. This structure determines a worker's trade union affiliation on the basis of his place of work.

The central trade union organization is the General Trade Union Confederation (GTUC). As of 1977 the combined membership in Rumanian trade unions was over 6.4 million workers in enterprises, institutions, and civic organizations. Collective farm workers are excluded from the provisions of the Labor Code and are not permitted to join the GTUC, a fact that was criticized in 1979 by the International Labor Organization's Committee of Experts on the Application of Conventions and Recommendations as a violation of ILO Convention 11, which Rumania has ratified. Rumanian trade unions represent workers at meetings with management, arrange the participation of workers in planned production, and are entitled to participate in drafting economic plans and labor legislation.

THE RIGHT TO FORM TRADE UNIONS

Article 27 of the Rumanian Constitution (as amended in March 1974) states that "The citizens of the Socialist Republic of Rumania have the right to associate themselves in trade unions and cooperative, youth, women's and sociocultural organizations." However, Article 3 of the Constitution circumscribes the independence of such unions by stating that "the leading political force in the whole of society is the Rumanian Communist Party." And Article 26 defines the Communist Party as "the highest form of political organization of the working class."

In addition, Section 164 of the Rumanian Labor Code states that "the unions are occupational organizations set up in virtue of the right of association laid down in the Constitution and operating on the basis of the bylaws of the General Trade Union Confederation, the federations for the different branches of activity, and the trade union organizations in the [economic] units." This section of the Labor Code therefore asserts that the

General Trade Union Confederation's bylaws are the only legitimate basis for all trade union activity.

A 1979 report of the International Labor Organization's Committee of Experts on the Application of Conventions and Recommendations notes this problem and states that "The Committee...had expressed the hope that to avoid any doubts regarding the scope of the provisions of Section 164 of the Labor Code, [a] new trade union act...should clearly establish unions, federations, and confederations which can clearly elaborate their own regulations and exercise their activities in complete independence from the General Trade Union Confederation. In this regard," the report continues, "the Committee considers that trade union unity imposed by law is contrary to the principle of formation by workers of organizations of their own choice and that, in all cases, diversity of trade unions ought to remain possible."

A test of the right to organize independent trade unions in Rumania occurred in 1979 with the formation of the Free Trade Union of Rumanian Workers (known by its Rumanian acronym, SLOMR).

In February 1979 SLOMR released its initial declaration. The independent trade union's founding document was signed by twenty individuals, sixteen of whom were workers from Turnu-Severin, a town in Southwest Rumania. The preamble of the SLOMR document asserts that the organization's right to exist is in full conformity with Article 22 of the International Covenant on Civil and Political Rights and with Article 8 of the International Covenant on Economic, Social, and Cultural Rights. Both articles were ratified by the Rumanian government in October 1974 and provide for freedom of association and the right to organize trade unions.

The SLOMR founding document clearly illustrates that the organization has the right to be considered a legitimate trade union organization. The document indicates that the principal goal of SLOMR is to struggle for respect for basic human rights in Rumania, and particularly for rights involving labor relations. In addition, the document states that "SLOMR militates for putting into effect...the right of every man to a sufficient standard of living, with respect to food, clothing, and habitation."

The basic focus of the SLOMR document is labor relations and labor conditions. The document asserts that unemployment is a widespread problem and asks for a lowering of work quotas, provision of free safety equipment and food, adequate safety precautions, and adequate heating and light in the workplace. It asks that workers' right to free time be respected and that compulsory, "patriotic" work be made optional.

The authors call on all workers denied their rights to notify the union of their particular field; they state that SLOMR "declares itself affiliated with the International Confederation of Free Trade Unions."

A March 6, 1979, SLOMR communique noted that 1,487 workers who had set up the clandestine Unofficial Trade Union of Workers, Peasants, and Soldiers of Mures County in 1978 sent representatives to visit Dr. Ionel Cana, founder of SLOMR, and proposed that the Unofficial Union be incorporated into SLOMR. In Tigru Mures, an industrial town which is the center of the Hungarian population of Transylvania, 1,000 inhabitants, one in every hundred adult residents of the town, registered their support of SLOMR.

On March 6, 1979, two days after the news of the SLOMR declaration was beamed into Rumania by Western radio stations, the telephones of two of the union's representatives, Dr. Ionel Cana, a physician, and Gheorghe Brasoveanu, an economist, were cut off. Other founding members were detained by the police. On March 10, Dr. Cana and Mr. Brasoveanu were arrested and according to Amnesty International were "said to have been confined to Jilava Prison Psychiatric Hopsital." Subsequently Dr. Cana was sentenced to a term of five and a half years' imprisonment. Nicolae Dascalu, another SLOMR member, was sentenced to eighteen months' imprisonment (reduced on appeal to ten months) under Article 94 of the 1974 Press Law, which prohibits disseminating information abroad without legal authorization. A number of other SLOMR members were sentenced to terms of imprisonment of up to six months on charges of "parasitism." SLOMR member Eugen Onescu was confined to a Bucharest psychiatric hospital for three weeks, and Father Gheorghe Calciu was arrested on March 10, 1979, and subsequently sentenced to ten years' imprisonment for his friendship with SLOMR founder Gheorghe Brasoveanu and for his involvement in the formation of the independent trade union.

Vasile Parashiv, a chemical worker from Ploesti, who had in 1971 called for a new law which would recognize that "trade unions are free, independent working class organizations which are accountable for their activity only to the workers who elected them and whom they represent," was arrested in Bucharest in February 1979, where he had traveled to indicate his support for the Free Trade Union of Rumanian Workers. According to Amnesty International, Paraschiv "was reportedly beaten, accused of being a member of Al Fatah, and subsequently released. Since then he has not corresponded or communicated with friends and relatives abroad, and it is feared that he may once again have been forcibly confined."

In 1976 Paraschiv was confined to a psychiatric prison hospital where he was diagnosed as suffering from psychopathic paranoia after he had protested injustices at his place of work to Communist Party authorities.

THE DEFENSE OF WORKERS' RIGHTS BY OFFICIAL TRADE UNIONS

Section 169 of the Rumanian Labor Code asserts that "Trade union organizations defend the rights of their members under labor legislation...." But Section 165(1) of the Labor Code likewise asserts that "The trade unions mobilize the masses for implementing the program of the Rumanian Communist Party for the building of a new society, and to this end carry on sustained activities for raising labor productivity, improving the quality of production, promoting technical progress, raising levels of training among the workers, promoting strict discipline in production and fulfillment by each worker on the staff of his obligations."

Thus, the Labor Code's assertion that trade unions must play a role in raising labor productivity and labor discipline creates an obvious conflict with their role as defenders of workers' interests.

Additionally, Section 12 of the Labor Code states that "workers are guaranteed the right to...working conditions in which occupational safety and hygiene measures safeguard life and health...." Despite this regulation, a number of serious accidents have occurred at workplaces in the last several years. On October 31, 1978, a violent explosion at the Pilesti petrochemical plant killed nine and wounded an unspecified number of people. Other accidents are known to have occurred at the Steagul Rosu plant in Brasov and the Danubiana auto-tire factory. The official General

Trade Union Confederation is not involved in investigating such accidents; moreover, such accidents are not even reported in the mass media or by the trade union press.

Despite the fact that Section 169 of the Labor Code states that trade unions "defend the rights of their members," there is no known instance of an official Rumanian trade union or the GTUC either interceding on behalf of a member of the independent SLOMR group or of workers who have been imprisoned or repressed for engaging in strikes. Nor does the GTUC have a history of protesting labor conditions.

Under such circumstances, it is fair to conclude that Rumanian trade unions side with the interests of the management of a workplace and with the interests of the government and do not effectively defend the rights of workers.

THE RIGHT TO STRIKE

Neither the Rumanian Constitution nor the Rumanian Labor Code guarantees the right to strike. Indeed, there is no mention of strikes in Rumanian legislation. As in other Eastern European states calling themselves "socialist," there is an implicit ideological bias against strikes. For instance, according to the Rumanian Labor Code, Section 1 (1): "In the Socialist Republic of Rumania, the abolition for all time of exploitation and oppression of man by man, the rapid development of forces of production, and the generalization of socialist production place labor—the principal factor in progress and civilization—in the highest rank of social values." This legislation, which asserts that exploitation and oppression have been eliminated, implies that strikes and other forms of worker protest are unnecessary.

Moreover, Article 100 (1) of the Labor Code, states that "Any culpable breach of obligations (including norms of conduct) by a person appointed to a work staff...constitutes an infringement of discipline punishable as appropriate and, as provided by law, with a) reprimand; b) warning; c) forfeiture of one or more increments on the wage scale; d) reduction of wages and reduction of allowances...for a period to three months; e) demotion...for a period of one to three months; f) disciplinary termination of a labor contract."

Article 29 of the Rumanian Constitution likewise contains a provision which can be interpreted as prohibiting the right to strike. It states: "The freedom of speech, press, reunion, meeting, and demonstration cannot be used for aims hostile to the socialist [system] and to the interests of the working people."

Since the signing of the Helsinki Accords in 1975, there has been only one instance of detailed information about a strike reaching the West—the Jiu Valley coalminers' strike of 1977. It provides an illustration of how Rumanian authorities deal with this form of worker protest.

On August 1, 1977, 35,000 coalminers began a strike in the Jiu Valley, site of Rumania's largest coalfield. Discontent revolved around a new pension law, overtime that had remained unpaid since March of that year, poor housing conditions, and grievances over inadequate food. Rumanian President and party General Secretary Nicolae Ceausescu dispatched Labor Minister and General Trade Union Confederation head Gheorghe Pana to the region, but the striking workers reportedly took Pana hostage and demanded that Ceausescu himself come to the Jiu Valley. When the Rumanian head of state arrived, he reportedly received a hostile reception, and when he was finally allowed to speak, he promised that no retaliatory measures would be taken against striking workers.

The strike indicated the widespread dissatisfaction of workers with the Rumanian government's long-standing policy of large investments in order to bolster the highest rate of growth in Eastern Europe at the expense of consumer goods and a higher living standard.

The strike resulted in some immediate concessions involving food supplies, a shortening of the workweek, and improvements in housing conditions.

Despite Ceausescu's promise that no retaliatory measures would be taken against the strikers, according to reports from a number of sources, up to four thousand strikers were later dismissed from their jobs, and many were transferred to other mines. Members of a twenty-person delegation that traveled to Bucharest to state the grievances of the strikers before the Central Committee of the Rumanian Communist Party were arrested upon their return to the Jiu Valley and sent without trial to work in districts where they were demoted and put under police surveillance.

Rumanian government and trade union officials denied that there had been a strike but admitted that "problems" existed in the Jiu Valley.

According to Amnesty International, "the miners [who were] banished" have been assigned to low-standard housing, described as "barracks." Two strike leaders, Ian Dobre and an engineer named Jurica, died shortly after the strike in circumstances which were never fully investigated by the police.

INTERNAL UNION DEMOCRACY

According to Section 166 of the Rumanian Labor Code, "Through all their activities the trade unions contribute to the development of a socialist consciousness among those who work, in line with the materialist conception of the world and society, and to the growth of moral attitudes in line with socialist and communist principles and equity."

Moreover, Article 165 (1) indicates that trade unions bear a responsibility for mobilizing "the masses for implementing the program of the Rumanian Communist Party." According to the Rumanian Constitution, the Communist Party "achieves an organized link with the working class" through "mass organizations," trade unions among them.

Section 165 (2) of the Labor Code indicates that "Trade unions have representatives on workers' councils and in government."

The subservience of Rumanian trade unions to the Communist Party and their participation in government lead to a denial of trade union independence and internal union democracy.

A new trade union law, which was to have replaced a 1944 law, has apparently been scrapped and was not even mentioned at the 1976 General Trade Union Confederation Congress despite the fact that in 1971 President Ceausescu had indicated that the 1944 law was outdated and outmoded.

Furthermore, the bureaucratization of trade unions, which was denounced in 1971 by Ceausescu, has not been overcome. Rather it has increased and at the 1976 General Trade Union Confederation Congress the proportion of persons directly employed in material production who were elected to the trade union bodies declined.

A telling illustration of the role of trade unions as instruments of the party and government is the fact that while in 1976 Gheorghe Pana was first elected GTUC chairman and only subsequently appointed minister of labor, by February 1979, even this superficial separation between the government and the GTUC was eliminated. Emil Bobu succeeded Pana in both posts simultaneously, and is today both a member of government and the country's leading trade union official.

The Constitution itself (Article 27) asserts that "through the mass and public organizations [including trade unions], the Rumanian Communist Party achieves an organized link with the working class, the peasants, the intelligentsia, and other categories of working people, mobilizing them in the struggle for the completion of the building of communism."

Thus the domination of the trade unions by the Communist Party is enshrined in the Constitution. The independent trade union activists of SLOMR affirm their own independence, contrasting it implicitly with the subservience of their country's official trade unions to the Communist Party. SLOMR, they wrote in their founding statement, "exercises its activities freely and is not a conveyor of any political force."

ANTI-WORKER MEASURES

Incarceration of independent trade union activists in psychiatric hospitals and prisons, banishment, and arrest and harassment of strike leaders have been considered in previous sections of this study. This section discusses other measures which can be characterized as anti-worker, and which are applied in Rumania.

Rumanian Labor Law includes strict provisions concerning labor discipline. Section 10 (parts 1 and 2) of the law states:

> The planned development of the national economy based on a high level of social organization of labor makes it necessary to establish labor relations on the principle of willing acceptance and consistent application of standards of socialist work discipline. Strict obedience of order and discipline is a basic obligation of every member of the worker body....
>
> The worker body, being aware that any act of indiscipline is prejudicial to work results and its own interest, has both a right and a duty to adopt a firm attitude toward any breach of labor discipline, and to call where necessary for the expulsion from the worker body of those who infringe order and discipline and fail to perform alloted tasks.

Articles 103-109 of the Labor Code, as well as Article 100 (1), which was cited above, codify the forms of punishment to be meted out for breach of labor discipline and for losses caused to the workplace and production schedule.

Article 5 of the Constitution, which describes work not simply as a right but as a "duty of honor," contains within it a clear element of compulsion. Furthermore, Article 18 of the Constitution, which guarantees the right to work, says nothing about the workers' right to choice of work. In addition, the Constitution does not provide for freedom of movement or choice of residence.

Additionally, Rumania has violated its obligations under International Labor Organization Convention 29, concerning the abolition of forced labor, which it ratified in 1930, and which the Communist regime has never revoked. In 1973 Law 3 of the Penal Code was promulgated. The law provides for "corrective labor without loss of liberty" as an alternative to imprisonment. The penalty also entails serious limitations on the freedom of movement, and calls for reduction of wages and loss of holidays.

CONCLUSION

Since the signing of the Helsinki Accords, information concerning violations of workers' rights has been reaching the West with increasing regularity. This can be attributed not to a relaxation of restrictions on the flow of information or to a lessening of political repression, but rather to a marked increase in discontent among workers and the growth of dissent.

As this study demonstrates, workers' rights are being systematically denied in Rumania. Moreover, in the years since the signing of the Helsinki Accords, a further erosion has occurred in the already substantially limited independence of Rumanian trade unions. With the increasing ferment of Rumanian workers, repressions have likewise increased, and independent trade union activists and strike leaders have been imprisoned, placed under surveillance, forcibly resettled, and incarcerated in psychiatric hospitals.

Czechoslovakia

INTRODUCTION

The trade unions of the Czechoslovak Socialist Republic (C.S.R.) are organized in the Revolutionary Trade Union Movement (ROH), whose executive organ is the Central Council of Trade Unions. Subordinate to the Central Council and reflecting Czechoslovakia's federal character are the Czech Trade Union Council and the Slovak Trade Union Council. Approximately 6 million Czechs, Slovaks, and workers of other nationalities—organized in eighteen country-wide unions ranging in variety from the Metal Workers Trade Union to the Workers in Art, Culture, and Social Organizations Trade Union—belong to the Revolutionary Trade Union Movement, membership in which is compulsory.

According to the C.S.R. Constitution, "the Czechoslovak Socialist Republic is a socialist state founded on the firm alliance of the workers, farmers, and intelligentsia, with the working class at its head" (Article 1, paragraph 1). Moreover, "All power in the Czechoslovak Socialist Republic shall belong to the working people" (Article 2, paragraph 1).

To determine the extent to which the actual state of workers' and trade union rights corresponds to the ideal expressed in the Constitution requires, first, looking back to 1968 at the role of workers and trade unions in the liberalization of Czechoslovak society known as the Prague Spring. That year, after two decades of passivity, workers and trade unionists came to play a crucial reformist role in their country's factories and trade unions. First they organized workers' (or enterprise) councils, whose goal was to increase direct worker participation in the management of enterprises. And second they instituted a series of far-reaching changes in the Revolutionary Trade Union Movement that culminated in the adoption in March 1969 of a new Charter and statutes which included the right to strike. These gains in the status of workers and trade unions, however, were short-lived. The Warsaw Pact invasion in August 1968 marked the end of the Prague Spring, while the replacement of Alexander Dubcek with Gustav Husak in April 1969 signalled the beginning of "normalization"—the progressive abandonment of the 1968-69 reforms and the reversion to a repressive social and political system more in line with the U.S.S.R.'s requirements. In the process, a large number of trade union activists were purged, the workers' councils were dismantled, and independent worker and trade union activity was virtually eliminated. As a result, within this atmosphere of political and social repression, the more overt forms of worker unrest—such as strikes or dissidence—that have plagued Poland, Rumania, and the Soviet Union appear to have been almost completely absent in Czechoslovakia.

THE RIGHT TO FORM TRADE UNIONS

Czechoslovak legislation is very specific on the prominent, if not explicitly exclusive, role to by played by the Revolutionary Trade Union Movement in the C.S.R. labor movement. The Constitution, for example, enshrines the ROH in Article 5:

> For the development of joint activities, for full and active participation in the life of society and the state, and to ensure the exercise of their rights, the working people form voluntary associations, particularly the Revolutionary Trade Union Movement, cooperative, youth, cultural, physical training, and other organizations.

This prominence and its implications for independent trade union activity were precisely what the ILO Committee of Experts on the Application of Conventions and Recommendations found most disturbing in its general report to the 65th Session (1975) of the International Labor Conference on Czechoslovakia's observance of ILO Convention 87 (Freedom of Association and Protection of the Right to Organize). Thus:

> The Committee has previously observed that, under Article 5 of the Constitution, Act 37 of 1959, and the Labor Code of 1965, the only trade union organizations that appear to be recognized are the Revolutionary Trade Union Movement and its constituent units. The Committee has pointed out that even if workers could establish, as the government has explained, other trade union organizations, these could not exercise any trade union function, since the legislation allocates such functions exclusively to the Revolutionary Trade Union Movement and its basic units. Any other trade union organization that might be legally established could not function as such, since it would be unable—under the law—to further and defend its members' interests.

Finally, in direct reference to the absence of the right to form unions, the Committee observed:

> A situation of this kind does not appear to guarantee to the workers the right to establish organizations of their own choosing, able to carry on trade union activities. The Committee wishes to point out again that even if it may be in the interests of the workers to avoid a multiplicity of trade union organizations, unity imposed by legislation is contrary to the principles of the Convention.

THE DEFENSE OF WORKERS' RIGHTS BY OFFICIAL TRADE UNIONS

Act 37, dated July 8, 1959, "respecting the status of works committees of the basic organizations of the Revolutionary Trade Union Movement," enjoins the basic (enterprise) union organization to:

> discuss and solve on behalf of the communities of workers employed in the establishment and in accordance with the interests of society as a whole all problems affecting the workers' vital interests, and particularly all labor, social, health, and cultural problems, and . . . thereby ensure that within the establishment the workers participate directly in the development, administration, and supervision of the establishment's activities.

Although a trade union's independence of action and ability to defend unrestrained the rights of workers appear to be solidly established in Act 37, the foundations of this ability are seriously undermined by other, more fundamental legislation. Article 6 of the Constitution is quite explicit on the unions' ultimate accountability to a "guiding force" (Article 4) other than the workers: "The National Front of Czechs and Slovaks, into which the people's organizations [including the ROH] are associated, is the political expression of the alliance of the working people of town and country, led by the Communist Party of Czechoslovakia."

Of more immediate interest to the workers of Czechoslovakia is that ROH subordination to the state and party apparatus visibly affects the ability of trade unions to defend workers' rights and interests. Calling the official unions "appendages of the economic apparatus," Professors Jan Patocka and Jiri Hajek, spokesmen for Charter 77, a human rights movement founded in 1977, argued in its Document No. 7 on Social and Economic Rights that:

> The unions do not ensure that broad layers of the workers take part in formulating wage policy either at the local or the overall level. They allow this policy to be decided from above; when the workers resist the lowering of wages...the unions do not stand by their side. If the workers go on strike...the unions betray them. Nor do the unions try to make the government work out the minimum necessary for existence, which could be adjusted each year, and which could form the basis for determining the minimum wage. The union organizations have at their disposal all kinds of information about the state of security of work and about the living conditions of the workers.... In none of these directions, however, do they bring pressure to bear for basic solutions. Instead of launching a struggle for participation in basic economic decision-making, they abandon the field and thus bear a common responsibility for bureaucratic decision-making.

Moreover, in cases where workers express political opinions disapproved by the Communist Party and thereby incur such forms of persecution as dismissal from work, the official trade unions not only refuse to speak out in their behalf, but also act as the disciplinary arm of the party by expelling the workers from their ranks. That this is a problem of potentially great proportions is evidenced by the fact that (as of late 1977) close to a third of the approximately nine hundred Charter 77 signatories were workers. Typical is the case of Jan Cutka, a mason and ceiling plasterer and signer of Charter 77, who received the following letter from the Central Council of Trade Unions:

> Article 5, clause (a), of the ROH statutes imposes the following obligations on its members: to defend and consolidate socialism; to consolidate the state's capacity to organize its defense; to consolidate the alliance with the Soviet Union and other socialist countries; and to work for progress, friendship, peace, and international cooperation in accordance with the principles of proletarian internationalism. For us to be able to grant legal aid to an ROH member, his attitude toward socialist society has to be a positive one. By signing the anti-state and anti-party pamphlet known as Charter 77 you have failed to comply with your duties as a member.

THE RIGHT TO STRIKE

Although strikes are not explicitly forbidden in the labor legislation of the C.S.R., the fact that the right to strike, which was formally included in the Charter and statutes of the ROH in March 1969, has since been removed, demonstrates the hostility of the Czechoslovak authorities toward this right.

In any case, the C.S.R.'s Labor Code makes very clear that a violation of "labor discipline" can result in immediate dismissal from work. According to Article 53 of the Code:

> An organization may terminate an employment relationship without notice in exceptional cases only, and then only...
> (b) if the worker has committed such a serious breach of labor discipline that his retention until the expiry of the period of notice is incompatible with the maintenance of labor discipline within the organization;
> (c) if the worker has endangered the safety of the state and his retention in the organization until the expiry of the period of notice is impossible without danger to the due performance of the organization's tasks.

"Socialist labor discipline," according to Article 72 of the Labor Code, "consists in the loyal performance by the workers of the obligations incumbent upon them as a result of their participation in the work of the community." The "loyalty" demanded by Czechoslovakia's "socialist" version of "labor discipline" clearly leaves no room for such "disloyal" actions as strikes.

INTERNAL UNION DEMOCRACY

The same trade union subordination to the Communist Party, as the "guiding force" in the C.S.R., that inhibits trade union defense of workers' rights also circumscribes the scope of possible internal trade union democracy. This is so first and foremost, because issues which conflict with the given party line are ipso facto ineligible for serious questioning and discussion. A second reason is that trade union and state and party apparatuses overlap to a degree that makes independent trade union decision-making even more problematic. For not only are numerous trade union functionaries Communist Party members, whose allegiance is first to the party and only then to the workers, but also many trade union officials occupy responsible positions in the party and in such basic units of C.S.R. government as the "people's committees."

Moreover, as Professors Patocka and Hajek wrote in Charter 77's Document No. 7, because "what is given first priority is not production but the need to protect and maintain the regime,""the economic and management system is deformed by being filled with people who are part of the apparatus of political power," and "especially members of the Communist Party." The effect on the unions, according to Patocka and Hajek, is that "it is not the blue- and white-collar workers but economic and other apparatuses which make the decisions."

Finally, the absence of a secret ballot at union elections and other voting occasions guarantees that trade union power will continue to reside undisturbed in the hands of the party and "economic and other apparatuses" already in control of the unions.

ANTI-WORKER MEASURES

Czechoslovakia's anti-worker measures are primarily directed against politically active worker dissidents. However, in light of the large number of workers who signed Charter 77 and of all workers' systematic refusal to join party-directed campaigns against the human rights movement, the number of workers liable to anti-worker persecution is probably quite large.

Among the first penalties encountered by a politically "unreliable" worker is wage discrimination. Second, should the dissident worker step too far out of line and violate "socialist labor discipline" by endangering the "safety of the state," he can be and usually is dismissed without notice on the basis of Article 53, section c (see above), of the Labor Code. Finally, the dissident worker will probably be placed on a blacklist, making it very difficult, if not impossible, for him to find suitable and/or steady employment. What awaits him then is best described by the Czech dissident and former Prague Spring party reformer, Zdenek Mlynar:

> People who are sacked for political reasons in Czechoslovakia find themselves in the following situation:
>
> They will not receive any other work, apart from unskilled temporary work, like unloading freight cars, etc.; they will not be able to enter into short-term working agreements or receive permission to carry out any free occupation without a prior hint from the relevant political apparatus.
>
> They have no right to any unemployment benefits, since this does not exist at all in Czechoslovakia, there being no unemployment.

> They cannot, however, live through support given in solidarity by individuals or groups of citizens, since this would be to abet the crime of parasitism, so that those who organized this support would be exposed to various forms of persecution.

Commenting on the C.S.R. government's defense of such anti-worker practices, the ILO Committee of Experts on the Application of Conventions and Recommendations concluded with reference to ILO Convention 111, Discrimination (Employment and Occupation), that "the measures authorized by the Convention in connection with the security of the state or the requirements of certain jobs should not be applied in such a way as to conflict with the basic protection provided by the Convention against discrimination in respect of employment on the grounds of political opinion."

CONCLUSION

In Czechoslovakia, more than in most Eastern European states, internal developments are greatly dependent on relations with the Soviet Union. Increased internal relaxation and fulfillment of the workers' rights outlined above are, therefore, very unlikely so long as the Soviet military and political presence in Czechoslovakia remains as prominent as it currently is. However, such a state of affairs need not preclude greater worker participation in reform movements. Indeed, the extent of worker involvement in Charter 77 clearly shows that Czechoslovak workers understand that their support is vital to the attainment of change, however minimal, in their country. The logical and probably inevitable next step for the workers of Czechoslovakia, therefore, would appear to be to engage in independent worker action and self-organization on the model of the free trade unions in Poland, the U.S.S.R. and Rumania with the hope of achieving even the limited improvements in working conditions potentially attainable by these means.

Appendix

Documents of Workers' Struggles in Eastern Europe

U.S.S.R. Documents

Charter

of the Association of Free Trade Unions of Workers in the Soviet Union. Effective from January 1, 1978 to January 1, 1979.

The Charter of the Association of Free Trade Unions is dated February 1, 1978. Source: AFL-CIO Free Trade Union News, May 1978.

Part One. Membership of the Association of Free Trade Unions of Workers in the Soviet Union

1. Membership in the Association of Free Trade Unions is open to any worker or employee whose rights and interests have been unlawfully violated by administrative, governmental, party, or judicial agencies.

2. A member of the Association of Free Trade Unions has the right to:

a. discuss freely all of the activities of the Association, make suggestions, and openly express and defend his opinions prior to the Association's coming to any decision

b. personally take part in meetings which pertain to his own activities or behavior

c. conduct a ceaseless battle for peace and friendship among peoples

d. raise the level of political consciousness

e. uphold the Charter of the Association of Free Trade Unions

f. carry out the social obligations with which he is charged by the Association

3. A member of the Association has the following advantages:

a. he receives proper legal counsel

b. he receives moral and material assistance from the Association to the extent to which it is available

c. he receives help in finding living accommodations, if such assistance is available, and helps his colleagues

4. Membership in the Association of Free Trade Unions is based on the individual's personal desire to join, with one week's time given for contemplation, because of the possible consequences

which may ensue as a result of his joining the Association.

5. Decisions regarding the acceptance of new members are made during Association meetings.

Part Two. Organizational Structure of the Association of Free Trade Unions of Workers

6. It is based on the principle of democratic centralism, which means:

a. everyone from the lower to the upper ranks is elected by the members of the Association and is accountable to them

b. all questions concerning the Association are decided in accordance with the Charter

c. decisions are made by majority vote

7. A free and businesslike discussion of questions concerning the Association of Free Trade Unions is an important principle of internal trade union democracy. Concepts of criticism and self-criticism, the activities and the initiative of Association members develop on the basis of this principle, and the level of consciousness and business discipline are strengthened by it.

8. The Association of Free Trade Unions is based on the association initially formed by the "forty-three" members.

9. The purposes of the Association of Free Trade Unions are:

a. to carry out the obligations reached by collective bargaining

b. to induce workers and other employees to join free trade union associations

c. to carry out those decisions of the Association which concern the defense of rights and the seeking of justice

d. to educate Association members in the spirit of irreconcilability toward deficiencies, bureaucracy, deception, inefficiency and wastefulness, and a negligent attitude to national wealth.

Part Three. Means of Support of the Association of Free Trade Unions

10. The Association of Free Trade Unions will depend on the following means of support:

a. monthly membership dues and contributions of unemployed members made within their means

b. dues which will comprise not over one percent of the working members' salaries and unlimited voluntary contributions

c. fees paid by non-members for legal services, the preparation and typing of complaints, etc., but the fees shall not exceed state tariffs

d. material aid received from foreign professional trade union organizations

Part Four. The Rights of the Association of Free Trade Unions as a Legal Entity

11. The Association of Free Trade Unions of Workers in the Soviet Union is a legal entity.

As soon as the Association of Free Trade Unions of Workers in the Soviet Union is recognized by the International Labor Organization or by professional trade unions of foreign countries, and after it has received moral and material support, it will review its Charter, keeping in mind the specific conditions of workers in our country. Such a review will be conducted not earlier than one year after the Association's founding.

Council of the "forty-three" members of
the Association of Free Trade Unions of Workers
in the Soviet Union
Moscow
February 1, 1978

[The Charter was signed by 110 persons, with a note stating, "there are a number of other colleagues who have asked that for the time being their names be withheld."]

APPEAL
To the International Labor Organization (ILO) and to Trade Unions in the West

The following appeal is dated February 1, 1980. Source: Labour Focus on Eastern Europe.

We are unemployed Soviet workers who have come to Moscow from various cities and republics of the country. Having no other possibilities, we are obliged to seek moral and material support with this Appeal through the Western press.

We have all been dismissed for exposing abuses or for speaking out against the management of enterprises where we worked. Among the issues we raised were pilfering and dilution of materials, bribery, a high rate of industrial accidents, and flagrant violation of the Labor Code.

We are middle-aged people (35-45 years old) with more than a decade of working experience. We have been deprived of work for periods of one to five years. At first we thought that our complaints would find support, if not at local level, then at least in higher institutions and the press.

On the one hand, the Soviet party and government call upon citizens to correct violations wherever they occur: in industry and in the life of the state and society. On the other hand, the authorities come down with special brutality on those who respond to propaganda appeals by strictly observing the regulations and speaking out in the interests of the enterprise.

All our attempts to achieve justice from government authorities have been in vain.

We appealed as individuals to the central organs of Soviet power: the Central Committee of the Communist Party of the Soviet Union, the Presidium of the Supreme Soviet, the Council of Ministers of the U.S.S.R., and the All-Union Central Council of Trade Unions. They did not reply to us.

The ruling organs decide our cases only in a one-sided manner: that is, they give bureaucratic answers and transfer us from one department to another. When we appeal to higher authorities, not only do they not take positive measures, but they apply unlawful methods against us for exercising our right to complain: on the pretext of registering us for an audience with the leadership, they seize us one by one and in groups, sending us to police stations and psychiatric hospitals.

This happens at the highest offices of power: in the reception rooms of the Central Committee of the CPSU, the Presidium of the Supreme Soviet, and the Procurator General's office.

It is impossible to be received in a single high Soviet institution. All highly placed personnel—our servants, as they like to call themselves—use the police to protect themselves from us.

We decided to unite. We began to act collectively. But just as before, they continue to expel us from Moscow with the help of the police and to put us in psychiatric hospitals.

Collectively, we addressed ourselves to all social, party, council, and trade union organizations; to the editorial offices of major newspapers: *Pravda*, *Izvestiya*, *Trud*, *Literaturnaya Gazeta* and to the magazines: *Ogonek, Kommunist, Partiinaya Zhizn,* and *Sotsialisticheskaya Zakonnost.* We received no reply.

We hoped that the new Constitution of the Soviet Union would rectify the lack of rights enjoyed by the working population. But the facts concerning repression and internment in psychiatric hospitals, which we present in this Appeal, prove that the new Constitution is not taken seriously by Soviet organs and that it merely serves as a screen with which to confuse the Soviet people and world opinion.

It was only after we made known these acts of arbitrariness and coercion that we were invited to the *Izvestiya* editorial office and to the KGB office. There, we were told, help had been promised.

But all this turned out to be a trick:

At the *Izvestiya* editorial office, they had only one aim. By taking us in one at a time, humoring us with promises, and bringing everything around to the name of the organizer, they did everything possible to sow discord among us.

In seeking to find out exactly how many people supported the collective complaint as well as their addresses, the KGB organs had the clear aim of exiling us from Moscow or placing us in psychiatric hospitals.

And so we decided to organize our own genuinely independent trade union. We did this in order to win the official and legal right to defend our interests—a right guaranteed by the Soviet Constitution—and to enlist in the common struggle for our rights other willing persons whose rights are unjustifiably violated.

We consider that only through a union of our own, basing itself on the public opinion of workers of all countries, can we force our government to respect the ordinary workers.

In our country there is no organ which objectively defends the workers' interests.

Soviet trade unions do not defend our rights and do not have the necessary authority. For key union posts are held by Communists —that is, by people who could not succeed in their party organizations. They are all technicians and engineers who, if not reelected for a new term, are again subordinate to one or another higher management official. And if only for these reasons, they always need to heed the opinions of top management.

Trade union elections take place in a purely formal manner: the chairmen of trade union committees are elected and appointed by the management of the enterprise, the party organizer, and the regional committee of the CPSU. According to the rules, one delegate per ten trade union members is elected to attend a conference whose purpose is to hear reports and elect new officials.

It is worth noting that, in the Soviet Union, there is not one enterprise with less than 100 percent trade union membership of the workers and technical-engineering employees.

All of this would be democratic, if only delegates were elected at a general meeting, in the presence of everyone. However, in order to secure support beforehand, the management and the party committee resort to the trick of having delegates elected by shop or section. Before this happens, there is a meeting of the technical-engineering personnel at which the trade union chairman and leaders of the party committee lay down how the election of delegates should be "carried out."

Afterwards the elections take place by section or shop. As a rule, the supervisor of the section or shop "recommends" (i.e., records) whichever candidates he likes. Out of gratitude to him they nominate him and the foremen, as well as someone from the technical-engineering staff. The employees elect their own delegates. The workers evidently do not get a look-in. In the end, although workers outnumber employees by ten, nearly all those who attend the conference are technical-engineering personnel—that is, those for whom workers' interests are not important.

The workers' delegates receive money that they do not have to return, and the buffets abound in normally scarce products and alcoholic drinks.

To the presidium are elevated, without any invitation, the enterprise management and representatives of the district (party) committee, the city trade unions, and the party organization. These then make a register of candidates, or in other words, they register on the ballot paper anyone they like.

No other candidates are registered. That is why the election of the incoming members of the trade union committee is ensured in advance.

The election of the chairman and the allocation of responsibilities take place at a table laden with food and spirits at public expense and to the cheers of clanging glasses.

The chairmen of lower trade union organizations go on to elect territorial trade unions, and so on.

In this Appeal we will substantiate our arguments with newspaper items confirming that these are not individual "shortcomings," but a normal part of everyday life. In its issue of January 27, 1978, *Leninskoye Znamya* [*Leninist Banner*—the organ of the Moscow provincial CPSU committee and Soviet of People's Deputies] carried an article "Getting Used to It" in its general column entitled "Following the anxious letters":

> ...For the second year running, the No. 3 administrative collective of the Mozhaiskovo Road building works has received a flood of anonymous letters to various local and district organizations... There were similar signs earlier... On October 14, 1977, there was a trade union meeting to review the work and hold elections. At the end of this, the workers were given a ruble each, while the office workers went to a restaurant to drink away trade union money... The enterprise manager, B. F. Stepakin [stated]: "We have an old tradition; we feel that it is better to drink collectively than to hide in a corner"... The chairman of the trade union committee, N. I. Miroshnikov, [said]: "The regional committee of the trade union puts aside special resources for such 'gatherings.' "

Trud (Labor) of January 20, 1978, published an article called "Strange Permits" from the town of Enakievo, Donetsk province:

> ...The statement of face-worker A. L. Todoseichuk from the platform of the election and review conference is understandable to many at the mine. A L. Todoseichuk severely criticized the chairman of the mine committee, V. S. Sigarev, for allowing violations of the Labor Code and for the improper allocation of material assistance. The worker brought forth concrete examples. He said: "Year after year, the same people use the privilege of sanitorium-resort treatment. Worse still: after absenteeism, D. Ganziuk was given a holiday; and soon after a stay in a sobering-up station, E. Litvin and A. Melikhov received permits [for accommodations at a rest home]. What is this? The managers of the mine, the general director of the Ordzhonikidze coal association, N. F. Semchenko, the secretary of the association's party committee, V. I. Gromov; and the chairman of the Enakiev territorial committee of coal industry trade unions, V.I. Kozlitin—all of whom are on the presidium, let this go by. The reaction was unexpected. A. L. Todoseichuk was a member of the mine committee. Previously he had been recommended for the new structure. But

> when it came to considering the candidates, the presidium did not nominate Todoseichuk. He was not included in the list for secret voting, even though this was proposed from the floor.
>
> Sigarev was again elected chairman of the mine committee, although out of 163 delegates at the conference only 59 voted against him. [The authors of the Appeal note that according to the rules, a two-thirds majority is required.] In broad daylight, in front of all to see, Sigarev was taken under protection, in spite of the opinions of those who openly spoke the truth about his improper conduct.
>
> A. L. Todoseichuk decided to fight for the truth. He wrote letters to the Donetsk regional and republic committees of the coal workers' trade union. He signed it with all his work-titles, face-worker, Communist, honored national miner, holder of the order of the Red Banner of Labor—but no one answered his letters.
>
> Sigarev forces signatures, sells holiday permits to a certain E. A. Sotnikova, who has nothing to do with the mine; as for the head librarian, N. I. Kuzmenko, he simply threw her out of his office (she had come to see him on official business); and the trade union chairman paid no attention to the official requests of the city procurator. After a short period of time in office, complaints appeared in several departments from Sigarev's subordinates. Each one mentions his rude behavior toward his associates. Because of this, people are leaving "of their own volition"...

In our previous open letters we wrote: "there are thousands of similar cases."

Yes, we did not exaggerate. We are convinced that every tenth worker or employee could fill our ranks.

Let us look at the press. *Pravda* of January 21, 1978, printed an article entitled "Insufficient Persistence":

> ...At the Petrozavodsk enterprise No. 1126 employing a thousand workers in the town of the same name, one-third of the workers left in the last year alone...

The newspaper *Evening Moscow* of January 21, 1978, carried an article "A Difficult Topic." Concerning the Sokol'nicheskii railway car repair and building works in Moscow, we read: "...We pay a great deal of attention to our work with cadres...What is the result? The balance is not in our favor, as 24 people left while 15 were hired..."

Leninist Banner of January 25, 1978, had an article entitled "Easy

Parting": "Over the past three years 262 workers have left the company. In effect, two out of three left..."

An article from *Pravda* of March 29, 1976, entitled "If a Labor Dispute Occurred":

> ...Legislation of the Armenian S.S.R. in particular, provides for punishment of violations such as abrogation of the labor contract with the management official or his removal from the occupied post. However, in our republic there has not yet been an occasion for the trade union to use this law. Meanwhile, all the same grounds for such sanctions are encountered..."

In the same article, not one-tenth of the incidents of groundless dismissal of workers and employees is mentioned; and not one of these received help from the trade unions.

Here is what happened in one large metallurgical factory in the city of Enakievo, Donetsk province, where there are more than 15,000 workers. To whom is their faith entrusted? *Pravda* of January 7, 1978, headlines "The Effectiveness of Criticism": "...The Director of the Enakievo metallurgical works, Iu. T. Cherneta, became so offended at criticism in the local paper that at the beginning of a meeting he put forward an ultimatum: 'Either me or her.' And he got what he wanted—the meeting did not begin until the 'her,' the reporter from the paper, left the hall..."

How do the newspapers write about the cream of the cream, that is, about Communists? *Pravda* of January 21, 1978:

> ...At an enterprise of 1,000 workers, 75 are Communists...The secretary of the party committee. A. Min'kowich, recently committed such a misdemeanor(?!?) that the Communists had to elect a new secretary, A. Ul'ianov. The Communists hoped that he would take matters in hand. But it did not work out: he didn't have enough character or experience. Furthermore, two other members had to be removed from the bureau: K. Asanov ended up in a sobering-up station and V. Ushanov violated financial discipline...

And then 49 wrote to *Pravda:* "The notice was not discussed in the brigades. There are no noticeable changes at the enterprise..."

The whole country is gripped in a corrosive mold of bureaucratism. This has been witnessed by us and by our comrades-in-misfortune, who have grown to over 200: We worked in various enterprises in over 150 different cities and regions of the country.

We are an insigificant part of the citizens who daily occupy the reception rooms of the central apparatuses.

We request the ILO and workers' trade unions to recognize our Association of Free Trade Unions of Workers and to give us moral and material support.

February 1, 1978

[This is followed by a list of 43 signatures to the Appeal as well as a list of 110 candidate members of the Association.]

A Statement to the International Confederation of Free Trade Unions Brussels, Belgium

The following statement was issued by the Free Interprofessional Association of Workers.

The Council of Representatives of the Free Interprofessional Association of Workers (SMOT), which was recently formed in the U.S.S.R., informs the ICFTU of its formation and wishes the ICFTU to accept SMOT into its ranks.

In January 1978 a group of workers led by the Donetsk miner Klebanov announced the formation of an Association of Free Trade Unions for the defense of workers' interests.

In spite of the massive repression against the independent trade union movement (including the Free Trade Union), the searches and arrests of its active members, the independent movement in the U.S.S.R. exists, and at this moment has taken on the organizational form of the Interprofessional Association (SMOT), incorporating within it the Free Trade Union and the Independent Trade Union, which was formed after Klebanov's arrest.

Under conditions of the totalitarian system, the trade union movement is forced to take on the form of a federation of autonomous trade union groups which appoint their representatives to a coordinating center—the Council of Representatives—which is the leading organ of the Interprofessional Association.

The Interprofessional Association has as its goal the defense of the economic, social, religious, and political rights of its members, as well as their day-to-day rights. It is an organization that provides mutual support in defense of workers' rights, gives mutual material aid to workers, propagates knowledge of laws, and offers all possible assistance to those who are not members of the Interprofessional Association.

Taking into account the error made by the Free Trade Union, we are not applying for membership in the ILO, to which entry by the Interprofessional Association is closed due to the stand taken by the ILO leadership in regard to any trade union that is independent of the All-Union Central Council of Trade Unions of the U.S.S.R.

In order that the activity of the Interprofessional Association be productive within the context of the ICFTU, we ask that you send us founding documents and literature describing the history and the contemporary state of the international trade union and workers' movement; literature reflecting the attainment of these movements and the contemporary legal and economic status of workers, as well as texts of those international, regional, and national agreements and covenants which touch upon these questions.

The Council of Representatives of the Free Interprofessional Association of Workers (SMOT): L. Agapova; V. Borisov; L. Volokhonsky; A. Ivanchenko; E. Nikolayev; V. Novodvorskaya; V. Skvirsky (arrested); A. Yakoreva.

A Letter from a Soviet Worker to AFL-CIO President George Meany

Vladimir Borisov, a founding member of the Free Interprofessional Association of Workers (SMOT) authored this letter in October 1978. In June 1980, following a period of intermittent incarceration for his trade union activities, Borisov was forcibly expelled from the U.S.S.R. Source: AFL-CIO Free Trade Union News, *April 1979.*

Dear Mr. Meany:

I would like to express to you my belated gratitude for the honor you have bestowed upon me by inviting me to the AFL-CIO convention. The Soviet authorities refused to give me permission to visit the United States, stating that the millions-strong working class of the United States does not have the right to invite me as a private person, and if it did have this right, then it could only do so through the All-Union Central Council of Trade Unions (VTsSPS), of which I am not a representative.

Indeed, not only am I not a representative of the VTsSPS, I am not even a member of this appendage of the state-party apparatus that the VTsSPS constitutes in our country. This is because I withdrew from this organization many years ago, when I became convinced that official trade unions in my homeland not only do not defend the rights of workers, but objectively facilitate the enslavement of the working class as well as the entire population. Under such circumstances I can place my sole hope on the new independent trade union and workers' movement which is undergoing its birth pangs.

Today this movement finds itself in a stage of formation, but the objective necessity for such a movement, its timeliness (which is expressed if only in the fact that its ideas are arising independently in the minds of many people scattered throughout the vast reaches of our homeland, ideas which are finding resonance in the hearts of many, despite our very low level of legal consciousness), strengthens the certainty that this movement will grow and become one of the decisive forces for bringing about significant change in our country. It is a movement that is capable of compelling the authorities to respect the rights of workers, as well as human rights in general.

But today, I repeat, our independent trade union and workers' movement is undergoing a very difficult period of formation, a period when the movement, without having yet grown strong, without having been able to stand firmly on its own two feet, is attacked by the full punishing force of the totalitarian state-employer, a state which is the exploiter and absolute monopolist in the realm of prices as well as wages. We are in a period when, one after another, the activists of our workers' movement are arrested and thrown behind prison bars or into special psychiatric prison hospitals.

Recently, on October 13, 1978, one of the most energetic activists of our independent trade union movement and a fighter for the revival of the workers' movement, Vladimir Skvirsky, was arrested on charges fabricated by the authorities. Having been humiliated by the trials of last summer [those of Aleksandr Ginzburg and Anatoly Shcharansky], the authorities decided not to confront him with political charges, but fabricated a trumped-up criminal case, in accordance with well-honed technique, as was done in the cases involving Malva Landa, Kirill Podrabinek, Felix Serebrov, Vladimir Slepak, Valeria Makayeva, and many others. A week before his arrest, Skvirsky was dismissed from his job after members of the KGB visited his supervisors. Since the late 1950s Vladimir Skvirsky has linked his personal fate with the struggle for human rights; he took part in the democratic movement and helped facilitate the birth of the workers' movement. Consequently, by arresting him the authorities have dealt a severe blow to the independent trade union movement.

This is a time of great difficulty for us, and I, as a person who bears a direct connection to the workers' and the independent trade union movements, turn to you and through you to the working class and the trade unions of the United States with a request that you give us active help. I turn to you with a call for international solidarity among workers.

Basing my observation on those scanty sources of information that we are able to glean at no small effort on the developments in world affairs and the ideological and political conflicts that are taking place, I have become increasingly convinced that in our struggle it is impossible to hope for the support of those political leaders and governments whose viewpoints and actions depend almost totally on the political, economic, and tactical gains of the moment, and whose blindness was so accurately noted by Lenin in 1921 (I have in mind the passage from Lenin's writings which you quoted during your testimony before the U.S. Senate Foreign Relations Committee, a quote which eloquently reveals the entire essence of the U.S.S.R.'s foreign policy and, in some measure, its internal policies in the decades ahead).

At the same time, I am convinced that the working class and the trade unions of the entire world are much more capable of soberly understanding the essence of events that are occurring throughout the world. The aspirations of trade union and workers' movements toward a solidarity among workers of all countries, toward a solidarity among peoples, which flows out of the very idea of the trade union, along with the struggle for the unfettering of the oppressed and the struggle for human rights in general, assure us that we will not stand alone.

Once again, I turn to you, as the representative of the largest trade union association in the United States, and through you to the workers of the entire world, with a call to solidarity, with a call to demonstrate your active help and support for the fledgling trade union movement in the U.S.S.R. I turn to you in the name of our freedom and yours, in the name of the implementation of workers' rights and of rights throughout the world.

Mr. Meany! Since I do not have the means for disseminating information, I ask you, in our name, to forward our appeal to the workers of all countries:

> Workers of the World!
> The governments of your countries, as your representatives, have concluded international agreements with the Soviet Union in the sphere of human rights, as well as in the area of workers' rights. Yet, they have shown themselves to be powerless in forcing the Soviet Union to honor its own obligations. They are much more interested in momentary political expediency, and for this sake they allow the precisely delineated international obligations assumed by Soviet party and state leaders to be turned into amorphous, and in no way binding, declarations!
>
> Compel the Soviet Union to respect *your own* rights, the rights given *you* by the obligations which the Soviet Union has assumed!
>
> We believe that you have greater strength, possibilities, and determination than your governments!
>
> Give your active support to the independent trade union movement in the U.S.S.R. and win the freedom of Vladimir Skvirsky and all arrested members of the workers' movement in my homeland!

For quite some time now, I have wanted to send you a simple, personal letter, but each time I sat down to do so, the immediate problems of our eventful life tore me away from my writing paper. These same circumstances have now compelled me to address an open, public letter to you, rather than a letter of a personal nature. Please try to understand and forgive me!

With profound respect for you and your long-lasting struggle for human rights throughout the world,

Sincerely yours,

Vladimir Borisov
October 1978

Polish Documents
The Strike Movement

The following article, written by members of the Social Self-Defense Committee (KOR) and by editors of the unofficial worker newspaper, Robotnik *(The Worker), on January 2, 1979, appeared in* Robotnik *in early 1979. Source:* Labour Focus on Eastern Europe.

Reports have reached the *Robotnik* of workers' strikes in many factories. Here are some data covering the last quarter of 1978.

From October 9 to 11 workers of the Pabianice dressing materials factory, ASO, went on strike. They were losing several hundred zlotys a month because a change of package sizes was introduced without any corresponding change in the scale of payments.

From October 10-14 workers of the Pabianice pharmaceutical factory, Polfa, went on strike because their bonus was withdrawn. The reason for this was that their factory's delivery plan was not fulfilled, although the production plans were met, and it was the management, not the workers, who were responsible for deliveries.

At the end of November workers of the Pabianice electric bulb factory, Polam, went on strike in protest against being deprived of a work-free Saturday. On December 1 the spinning room workers in the Technical Textiles plant in Pabianice went on strike. The reason was that an inferior-quality yarn was classified as top quality, and workers were deprived of a special bonus for working with inferior-quality yarn.

On October 26, 1978, workers of the confectionary plant, Optima, in Lodz went on strike, demanding a wage settlement. Their wages were reduced due to a lack of raw materials.

On November 18, 1978, workers of the concrete-mixing factory in Myszkow went on strike because their wages had not been paid on the appointed date.

On December 22, 1978, a violent protest broke out among the miners of the fifth division of the Gliwice mine against the twelve-hour working day and enforced work over Christmas holidays. Earlier (last summer) miners of the Rybnice and Upper Silesia coalfields protested against prolongation of working time.

Reports of strikes reach us by chance. We can assume that they illustrate only a fragment of a wider workers' movement in the whole country, for conditions in other factories are similar to those that caused workers' protests known to us.

The immediate cause of strikes is most often a wage reduction, increase of production norms not previously accepted by the workers themselves, cancelling of work-free Saturdays, or enforcing additional working hours (work on Sundays or 12-hour day on Saturdays). Managements try to save their threatened production plans by economizing on the workers' wages or looking for "reserves" in extension of working hours or productivity increases. Many plants have not fulfilled their plans as a result of numerous standstills in the second and third quarters of 1978, or did not work at full capacity, due to a lack of raw materials and energy, irregular supplies, bad organization and mismanagement in the whole of the economy.

Economic and political management on different levels is trying to lay the blame for the economic crisis on workers who are not responsible for it. This takes place at a time of a general fall in living standards (rising prices, "commercial" shops) and a deterioration in the supplies of foodstuff, in a situation which offers no prospects of change for the better in the living conditions of workers and their families.

All attempts at further lowering of workers' living conditions must meet with firm protest. All cases of workers' protests known to us had the same character: workers have been defending themselves against unjust wage reductions or exploitation. As an additional postulate they demanded improved supplies of goods to stores. They have not put forward new demands but merely defended what is theirs by right.

In the disputes between management and workers, the party-controlled trade unions defend the vested interests of the party-economic apparatus. And thus workers cannot count on the unions' support. A strike, or the threat of a strike, has become the only method available to defend workers' rights. On the whole, strikes last for a short time and end with a short-term success. The management refunds lost wages, restores former productivity norms, or reintroduces a work-free Saturday. For the most part, however, these concessions apply to individual cases only and take a form that does not satisfy the workers: for example, they are given a bonus instead of due wages and thus have no guarantee for the future. Food supplies that usually improve after a workers' protest also have a temporary character. Often, some time after the tense atmosphere is relieved, reprisals come for the active participants of the strike—they are dismissed from work or transferred to worse jobs.

A significant weakness of workers' protest actions so far has been a lack of solidarity with persecuted colleagues as well as the temporary character of the achievements won by the strikes. Therefore it is necessary that workers organize themselves in more permanent forms, such as strike committees or free trade unions. These in turn would represent workers in disputes with management, would see to it that the rights won by workers are respected, and would organize defense for the victims of repression.

The Social Self-Defense Committee, KOR, and *Robotnik* announce that they give help and will continue to give it to the persecuted worker activists. Our help involves: legal aid in case of deterioration in working conditions or dismissal; financial help in the form of unemployment benefits in case of dismissal and inability to find work elsewhere. This help is distributed by a workers' fund created from the contributions of workers and members of the intelligentsia and supported by the fund of the Social Self-Defense Committee, KOR.

The Social Self-Defense Committee, KOR, and the editors of *Robotnik* declare their intention to inform the public—since the official media keep silent about the strikes in our country—about all workers' protests confirmed by us. Please send in all confirmed information about strikes to members of KOR and the editors of *Robotnik*, in particular to:

Bogdan Borusewicz, Sopot, 23 marca 98 m 24.
Anka Kowalska, Warsaw, Estonska 4, tel. 17 53 07.
Jacek Kuron, Warsaw, Mickiewicza 27 m 64, tel. 39 39 64.
Jan Jozef Lipski, Warsaw, Konopczynskiego 4 m 9, tel. 27 34 72.
Jan Litynski, Warsaw, Al. Wyzwolenia 9 m 125, tel. 28 71 04.
Zbigniew Romaszewski, Warsaw, Kopinska 36a m 77, tel. 22 29 25.
Jozef Sreniowski, Lodz, Laurowa 2, tel. 73 470.
Henryk Wujec, Warsaw, Nesseberska 3 m 48, tel. 42 63 38.

Information sent in should include: name of town and factory, if possible the division and shift, the dates of beginning and end of the strike, its causes, demands put forward, the course of the strike, the number of strikers. Please supply detailed information about persons who held talks with the strikers, if and how their postulates were to be met, who suffered reprisals after the strike was over, and how and whether the workers' demands have been met.

All information received about strikes will be verified. It will be of great help if we receive addresses where details can be obtained. Unconfirmed reports cannot be published.

The Social Self-Defense Committee, KOR, and the editors of *Robotnik* will support peaceful forms of workers' self-defense. The policy of lowering living standards of the population and increasing exploitation does not help to overcome the economic and social crisis but, on the contrary, aggravates it.

Charter of Workers' Rights

The following Charter of Workers' Rights was initiated by the editors of Robotnik (The Worker), *an unofficial Polish biweekly, and was jointly prepared with other Polish worker activists. The Charter began to circulate in Poland in the summer of 1979 and was issued in a special edition of* Robotnik, *Number 35. Source:* Freedom Appeals, *November-December 1979.*

Because:

- citizens have been deprived of the right to participate in resolving matters that affect them
- the fundamental rights of working people, such as the right to safe and rational work, equitable pay, and the right to time off, have been limited
- social inequality and social injustice have been intensified
- there is an absence of institutions that defend working people, including the official trade unions
- workers have been deprived of their fundamental right to self-defense, i.e., their right to strike
- society must bear the full brunt of the costs of the errors committed by the authorities, as well as the general costs of the crisis

we have initiated actions whose long-range goal is the creation of a system of self-defense for working people, particularly the establishment of independent trade unions.

We would like to begin with problems whose resolution, in our opinion, seems possible, if only in part.

1. *Earnings*

At the very least, wages should increase at the same tempo as the cost of living; naturally, it is necessary to introduce a *cost-of-living supplement.*

Everyone should be guaranteed a *subsistence minimum;* groups of specialists should determine such a minimum and adjust it in accordance with the growth of prices; families that live below the minimum should be provided with appropriate compensations.

Efforts should be made to strive toward the liquidation of flagrant and unjustified wage differences.

Slowdowns, changes of norms, etc., cannot lead to the lowering of earnings.

Workers who carry out the same work under identical conditions should receive compensation in accordance with a unified rate, irrespective of the sector of the economy in which they are employed.

2. *Worktime*

It is impermissible to be forced to work overtime or to do supplementary and voluntary work; miners must be guaranteed days off on Sundays and holidays.

Everyone deserves the legal guarantee of *Saturdays off.*

Efforts must be made to introduce a *forty-hour workweek without a reduction in pay.*

3. *Work Safety*

Rules and norms concerning work safety must be *scrupulously enforced;* special commissions with wide-ranging powers, including the right to shut down enterprises, must oversee this; commissions controlled by the BHP (Health and Safety Code), commissions investigating accidents, and also doctors should be *institutionally independent* of the factory administration.

No one who loses his health as a result of harmful work conditions should be without his due compensation or pension.

It is necessary, at present, to establish a verification list of occupational diseases.

It is necessary to eliminate *night-shift work for women;* it is impermissible to allow women to carry out hard physical labor.

4. *Privileges*

The evaluation of a worker and his promotion cannot be dependent on his party membership or his political or philosophical convictions.

Awards such as prizes, apartments, or holidays must be allocated in an open manner; likewise, the principles governing the granting of such awards, as well as the names of recipients of such awards, should be made public.

It is necessary to eliminate the privileges of groups linked to the authorities (i.e., the militia, the party apparatus) and to eliminate other special awards such as apartments, construction supplies, automobiles, special hospitalization, luxury vacation homes, special retirement benefits, etc.

5. *Compulsion to Commit Acts Against One's Conscience*

No one can be forced to commit immoral acts; to become an informant in matters of concern to the Polish Workers' Party (Communist Party) or the state security service. No one can be forced to participate in attacks on innocent people.

It is impermissible for workers to engage in work which endangers their own safety and that of others, to conceal accidents, to give false testimony, etc.

6. *The Labor Code*

It is necessary to make fundamental changes in the requirements of the Labor Code of 1975, which introduced regulations not in the interests of workers. Its articles are not explicit, and therefore, individual situations can be, and often are, interpreted in accordance with the interests of management.

Concretely: it is necessary to amend Article 52, which is utilized as an anti-strike statute (it is on this basis that masses of workers were dismissed from their jobs after the strikes of June 1976); the right to strike must be *legally guaranteed*.

The management of the enterprise should explain in writing to every worker who is dismissed the reasons for his dismissal; the worker should continue at his job until a final resolution of his case has been reached at every successive level of the judicial process; through the entire course of the judicial process, the worker should have the right to legal counsel.

Elected workers' representatives should, likewise, be legally protected from dismissal for a certain period after the conclusion of their term of office.

We believe that the implementation of these postulates depends on our attitude. The fact that workers can win concessions from the government and management is demonstrated by the major strikes in 1956, 1970, and 1976, as well as by individual strikes.

For many months, we have borne the costs of the crisis on our backs: the steadily worsening equipment and roadways, the decline in wages, the rise in prices. In many factories the workweek has been lengthened, free Saturdays are being taken away from us, delays are on the increase. If we do not now begin to defend our own interests, our situation will continue to worsen.

Nonetheless, in order for us to win, it is necessary to rid ourselves of our sense of powerlessness, to cease the quiet endurance of further limitations of our rights and the worsening of our living conditions. It is necessary to search for the most effective forms of action. We have great possibilities.

1. Undoubtedly, the most effective course of action is strikes, even those on a small scale. In general, these are effective merely in the short run. In order not to negate the gains of a strike, it is necessary for its participants to elect representatives who are sensitive to the realization of their tasks. If workers are able to act in solidarity and are unafraid, it is possible to force management into making concessions by the very threat of a strike: through presenting petitions or sending delegations.

2. Much can be achieved simply by open publicity. It is necessary to speak and protest loudly when harm is being done to someone, when we see injustice. It is necessary to expose the activities of cliques and to uncover instances of privileges, carelessness, waste, the violations of BHP (Health and Safety Code), and the covering up of accidents. It is necessary to speak of such things to one's colleagues and at meetings. It is necessary to take stands against the authorities, to inform independent social institutions and the editorial boards of independent publications.

3. There are many problems at the workplace which can be resolved by making use of official trade unions. Certainly it would be better for us if these were not as inert as they usually are. It is necessary to demand that trade unions defend the interests of workers by utilizing trade union meetings for discussions, by pressing demands, by electing to the trade union leaders who will

implement such demands.

4. In order that our actions not be premature or uncoordinated, there is the constant activity of workers' groups. Such groups, at first not overtly, can formulate action programs, organize concrete activities, search for the general public's support, and in time announce the existence of independent workers' committees.

5. Where there is a strong, organized community of workers who are capable of protecting their representatives from work dismissals and arrests, it is necessary to create committees of independent trade unions. As the experience of working people in democratic Western countries shows, this is the most effective way of defending the interests of workers. Only independent trade unions, which have the support of the workers they represent, have a possibility of resisting the authorities; only they can constitute the force with which the authorities must reckon and deal on equal terms.

We the signatories of this appeal, obligate ourselves to act in the interests of the postulates listed in this Charter of Workers' Rights.

We are, likewise, creating a Mutual-Aid Fund and declaring that we will support it with regular dues. The assets contained in the fund are allocated to help those persons who are dismissed from work for participating in the activities of independent trade unions.

Addenda

Our activities are in accordance with the law. In ratifying the various international covenants and the International Labor Organization conventions, the government of the People's Republic of Poland has agreed to the following:

I. *Convention 87, Article 2, of the International Labor Organization, Freedom of Association and Protection of the Right to Organize. International Covenant on Economic, Social, and Cultural Rights,* Article 8, 1. (a) (The right of everyone to form trade unions and join the trade union of his choice).

II. *International Covenant on Economic, Social, and Cultural Rights,* Article 8, 1. (d) (The right to strike).

[This document was signed by sixty-two persons, including editors of *Robotnik,* numerous workers, and students. The signatures were gathered in twenty-three Polish cities.]

Founding Declaration of the Committee for Free Trade Unions in Katowice

The Committee for Free Trade Unions was founded in the Silesian city of Katowice on February 23, 1978. Source: Labour Focus on Eastern Europe.

Faced by the centralized and all-powerful apparatus of power, and faced by the complete dependence of the factory directors and trade union officials on this apparatus of power, we, the ordinary workers, are effectively isolated and weak. We are being exploited because greater and greater effort is constantly being demanded of us, yet the standard of living of ourselves and our families is not only failing to improve but is deteriorating. We are convinced that this situation will remain as long as we don't organize ourselves into independent trade unions. It is only by uniting that we will be able to effectively oppose the state apparatus and those in the party and the economy who are exploiting us...

We, workers and employees of Upper Silesia and the coalmining basin, are the first to form free trade unions.

We launch an appeal to the workers throughout Poland: create independent trade unions, build workers' committees which will organize united action for all of us. It is only by uniting and organizing our forces that we will have the possibility of escaping the exploitation that is oppressing us and of creating a better life for our families and for ourselves.

Committee for Free Trade Unions in Katowice
Bogdan Cygan, Wodzislaw Slaski; Roman Ksciuszek, Myslowice-Kosztowy; Wladyslaw Sulecki, Gliwice; Kazimierz Switon, Katowice.
February 23, 1978

Leaflet by Katowice Committee

Workers and employees of Upper Silesia and the coalmining basin:

We have the right to rest after work, we have the right to a family life, to spend time in our homes. Unhappily, this right is systematically denied to us. In a number of factories, Sunday working is obligatory. "Activities for society and the party" are also compulsory, and in reality they are simply a means of using our labor power without payment—another symptom of our exploitation.

It is up to us alone whether this exploitation will continue. All of us must demand more and more firmly that the state and economic authorities promise us:

- The forty-hour work week
- The right to complete rest on Sundays

In our struggle for workers' rights and for those of employees, we are not alone. The whole of society supports us. We are supported by the democratic opposition and especially by the Movement for the Defense of Human and Civil Rights. The voice of the Church is particularly important.

All those who have been or are still being mistreated can address themselves to the Committee for Free Trade Unions in Katowice. Its address is: Katowice, 30 Mikolowska Street, Flat 7 (the same address as that of the information and consultation office of the Movement for the Defense of Human Rights). Within the limits of our capacities we will try to help those who are being mistreated. You can also write directly to the members of the committee who have signed below.

The Committee for Free Trade Unions in Katowice
B. Cygan, R. Kscuiszek, W. Sulecki, K. Switon

Founding Declaration of Baltic Committee

The Founding Committee of the Free Trade Unions of the Baltic Seaboard was founded in the port city of Gdansk on April 29, 1978. Source: Labour Focus on Eastern Europe.

The true Polish trade union movement ceased to exist thirty years ago.

Forced dissolution of political parties, such as the PPS (Polish Socialist Party), the PSL (Polish Peasant Party), and other independent organizations representing various social groups in the country, preceded by the imposed merger of individual labor unions into a single (state-controlled) body, resulted in the trade unions becoming yet another institution representing the interests of a monopolistic state employer, rather than of the employees. The unions became an extension of the political structure of the ruling Polish United Workers' Party and a pliant administrative device to operate a system of organized exploitation of all social groups in Poland.

A population deprived of its natural and necessary forms of self-defense could only react impulsively: violent eruptions of social discontent—such as in Poznan in 1956[1] during the "March Events" of 1968[2], the Baltic Coast workers' revolt of 1970[3], and lastly in June 1976[4]—were always associated with a menacing danger of a major revolution of unpredictable national and international consequences.

The [party] authorities, though occasionally forced to retreat, as in June 1976, or to offer a tactical and temporary appeasment, as in 1956 and in December 1970, proved to be incapable of introducing any form of democratization of public life. Such incapacity resulted in a constantly aggravated social and economic crisis, leading to a crisis of state authority.

What is needed today is a process of widespread democratization. The population must continue to strugge for a democratic form of government. All social strata should regain their right to self-determination and be allowed to recreate social institutions, through which their rights could be truly implemented.

Only free unions and associations can save the state, since only the process of true democratization can lead toward the integration of the interests and the will of the citizen with the interests and the authority of the state. These tasks are being carried out presently by existing [dissident] social institutions, such as the Social Self-Defense Committee, KOR[5], the Movement for the Defense of Human and Civil Rights[6], the Society for Academic Courses[7], and the Students' Solidarity Committees[8].

While remembering the tragic events of December 1970 and acting in compliance with the expectations of numerous groups and milieus of the Baltic Coast region, we wish to follow the lead of our Silesian colleagues[9] by organizing independent labor unions in our area.

Today, on the eve of May Day, which for over eighty years has symbolized the struggle for workers' rights, we hereby call into being the Founding Committee of the Free Trade Unions of the Baltic Seaboard.

The aim of the Free Trade Unions is to create an organized form of defense of economic, legal, and humanitarian interests of the working population. The Free Trade Unions declare their willingness to assist and to protect all employees, irrespective of their political views or their qualifications.

The Founding Committee will operate openly through their representatives, leaving our collaborators and supporters the right of decision and voicing their opinions.

Whereas we wish to identify ourselves with the guiding principles of the (unofficial) journal *Robotnik*[10], we shall express our views in its columns, or in our own publications. We shall also inform our readers about the progress of our activities and our achievements.

We appeal to all working people—the workers, the technical, managerial, and administrative staff: form your own independent employee representation committees. Alternatively, you may reach the same goal by introducing independent-minded activists into your works councils—people who would represent the electorate's interests in a true and honest manner. We would like our initiative to become a stimulus for a number of individual, varied, and independent social actions.

We appeal to independent social institutions for support and for the widest publicity for our initiative.

We appeal to all for solidarity in the struggle for a brighter future.

For and on behalf of the Founding Committee
Andrzej Gwiazda—Gdansk, ul. Wejhera 3c, apt. 118
Krzysztof Wyszkowski—Gdansk, ul. Pomorska 14b, apt. ??
Antoni Sokolowski—Gdansk, Poland
April 29, 1978

Footnotes

1. In June 1956 attempts to suppress a workers' demonstration in the Polish industrial city of Poznan led to a full-scale working-class uprising and an open political crisis during which Gomulka came to power.
2. In March 1968 a mass student revolt was used as the pretext for sweeping repressive measures against Polish intellectuals and Jews.
3. A package of price rises provoked mass strikes on the Baltic coast in December 1970. When the police and the army responded by shooting down workers, the discontent spread and Gomulka was removed from power, Edward Gierek, the present party leader, taking his place.
4. In June 1976 Gierek's attempt to introduce large price increases was stopped

by widespread workers' strikes and protests.
5. The Social Self-Defense Committee, KOR, was established in the autumn of 1977 as a civil rights organization, replacing the KOR (Polish initials for the Workers' Defense Committee) which was set up the year before specifically to campaign against repression of workers who had engaged in the June 1976 strikes and protests.
6. The Movement for the Defense of Human and Civil Rights was established in the spring of 1977. It publishes a journal called *Opinia*.
7. The Society for Academic Courses is an unofficial university established late in 1977 to provide lectures and discussions on history, politics, philosophy, etc.
8. The Students' Solidarity Committee (SKS) was formed in May 1977 after the death of a student civil rights activist, Stanislaw Pyjas, in Krakow. Local committees have since been formed in other university towns.
10. *Robotnik (The Worker)* is an unofficial journal started in late 1977, which claims a monthly circulation of between 10,000 and 20,000.

Agreement Between the Government Commission and the Interfactory Strike

This is the text of the agreement concluded by the Interfactory Strike Committee and the Polish government which was the culmination of the wave of strikes in July and August, 1980. The agreement was signed on August 31, 1980, and was published in Glos Pracy, *the journal of the official trade union organization, on September 2.*

Having examined the 21 demands submitted by the striking work forces, the government commission and the Interfactory Strike Committee adopted the following decisions:

With regard to point one that states: "To accept free trade unions independent from the party and employers as provided for by ILO Convention 87, which was ratified by the Polish People's Republic and which concerns trade union freedoms," it was agreed:

1. The performance of trade unions in the Polish People's Republic does not fulfill the hopes and expectations of employees.

It is considered expedient to establish new self-governing trade unions that would genuinely represent the working class. No one will have his right to remain in the present trade unions questioned and it is possible that the two trade unions will establish cooperation in the future.

2. In view of the establishment of new, independent and self-governing trade unions the Interfactory Strike Committee declares that they will observe the principles laid down in the Constitution of the Polish People's Republic. The new trade unions will defend the social and material interests of employees and do not intend to play the role of a political party. They approve of the principle that production means are social property—a principle that is the foundation of the socialist system in Poland. Recognizing that the PZPR plays the leading role in the state and without undermining the actual system of international alliances, they seek to ensure for the working people suitable means of control, of expressing their opinions and of defending their interests.

The government commission declares that the government will guarantee and ensure the complete respect for the independence and self-governing of the new trade unions both as regards their organizational structure and their performance at all levels of activity. The government will ensure for the new trade unions all opportunities for fulfilling their basic functions in defending the interests of employees and implementing their material, social and cultural needs. At the same time, the government guarantees that the new trade unions will not be subjected to any discrimination.

3. The establishment and activity of the independent, self-governing trade unions are consistent with ILO Convention 87 which concerns trade union freedoms and the defense of trade union rights, and ILO Convention 98 which concerns the right to associate and the right to collective negotiations. Both conventions have been ratified by Poland. The diversity of trade union and employee representations will entail suitable legislative amendments. In this connection the government pledges to make legislative proposals concerning in particular the law on trade unions, the law on workers self-government and the labor code.

4. The established strike committees can, if they want, transform themselves into factory employee representation bodies such as workers' committees, employees' committees, workers' councils or the founding committees of the new self-governing trade unions.

As the founding committee of those trade unions, the Interfactory Strike Committee is free to choose the form of a single union or association within the coastal region.

The founding committees will function until new authorities are elected in accordance with the statutes.

The government pledges to create the conditions for the registration of the new trade unions outside the register of the Central Trade Union Council.

5. The new trade unions should enjoy genuine opportunities for publicly evaluating the key decisions that determine the working people's working conditions: the principles of dividing the national income into consumption and accumulation, the distribution of the social consumption fund for various purposes (health, education, culture), the basic principles of remuneration and the lines of wage policy—particularly the principle of an automatic adjustment of wages under conditions of inflation, long-term economic plans, investment policy and changes in prices.

The government pledges itself to ensure conditions for the exercise of these functions.

6. The Interfactory Committee ["strike" is omitted] establishes a center for social and labor studies, whose task will be to objectively analyze the employees' situation, the working people's living conditions and the ways of representing employees' interests. The center also will prepare expert opinions on the wage and price indexes and will propose forms of compensation. It also will publish the results of its research. In addition, the new trade unions will have their own publications.

7. The government will ensure that the provisions of Article 1, Paragraph I, of the 1949 trade union law that stipulate that workers and employees are guaranteed the right to voluntary association in trade unions are observed in Poland. The new trade unions will not join the association represented by the Central Trade Union Council. It is agreed that the new law will preserve this principle. At the same time, representatives of the Interfactory Strike Committee or of the committees that will found the self-governing trade unions and representatives of other workers bodies will be ensured participation in formulating this law.

With regard to point two that states: "To guarantee the right to strike and to guarantee security for strikers and for persons helping them," it was decided:

The right to strike will be guaranteed in the trade union law now under preparation. The law should define the conditions under which a strike is proclaimed and organized, the methods of settling disputed problems and responsibility for violating the law. Articles 52, 64 and 65 of the Labor Code cannot be applied with regard to the participants in a strike. Also, the government guarantees for strikers and for the persons helping them personal security and the maintenance of prevailing working conditions until the law is passed.

With regard to point three that states: "To observe freedom of speech and the printed word, that is, not to repress independent publications and to make mass media available to representatives of all religions," it was decided:

1. Within three months the government will introduce in the Sejm a draft law on control of the press, publications and entertainment—based on the following principles. Censorship should protect the interests of the state. This means the protection of state and economic secrets, the extent of which will be more closely defined by legal enactments, and the protection of the state's security matters and important international interests. This also means the protection of religious beliefs and, at the same time, of the belief of nonbelievers and the prevention of spreading matter that is harmful to morals. This draft law would also deal with the right to appeal to the supreme administrative court against the decisions of the organs responsible for control of the press, publications and entertainment. This law will be enacted through modifications to the Administrative Procedure Code.

2. The issues of the use of the mass media by religious associations with regard to their religious activities will be effective through agreement between state bodies and the interested religious associations on substantive and organizational problems. The government will ensure that the radio will transmit a Sunday Mass under a detailed accord with the Episcopate.

3. Radio, television, the press and publications should be used to express the plurality of ideas, views and judgments. This use should be subjected to social control.

4. Like the citizens and their organizations, the press should be able to have access to public documents (acts), especially administrative documents, socioeconomic plans and so on, issued by the government and its administrative bodies. The exceptions to the principle of the openness of the administration's activities

will be defined in the law as stipulated in Point One (above).

With regard to Point Four that states: "a) To restore the former rights of the people dismissed from their jobs for the strikes in 1970 and 1976—the students banned from higher schools for their convictions: b) to free all political prisoners (including Edmund Zadrozynski, Jan Kozlowski and Marek Kozlowski); c) Abolish repressions for convictions," it was decided:

a. To examine immediately the correctness of the dismissals from jobs for the strikes in 1970 and 1976. In all cases raised, if irregularities are ascertained, to immediately restore the jobs to the people concerned, provided they want to have them back, and to take into account the qualifications they have acquired in the meantime.

A corresponding procedure will be used in the case of the students banned from higher schools.

b. To refer the cases of the persons mentioned in point b) (above) to the minister of justice who will examine them and will within two weeks institute the necessary proceedings: In the cases in which the listed persons are deprived of freedom, their punishment will be interrupted until the proceedings are completed.

c. To examine whether there is any justification for temporary arrest and to set free the persons mentioned in the annex.

d. To fully observe the freedom of expressing one's convictions in public and professional life.

With regard to Point Five that states: "To publish in the mass media the information about the establishment of the Inter-factory Strike Committee and to publish its demands," it was decided:

This demand will be fulfilled by publishing this protocol in national mass media.

With regard to Point Six that states: "To take genuine action in order to extricate the country from its crisis situation through a) fully informing the public about the socioeconomic situation, and b) enabling all social communities and sections to participate in the discussion about the reform program," it was decided:

We deem it necessary to greatly accelerate the work on economic reform. The authorities will outline and publish the basic tenets of this reform within the next few months. It is necessary to ensure that the public discussion of this reform is extensive. In particular, the trade unions should participate in formulating the laws on socialist economic organizations and on workers self-government. The economic reform should be based on radically increased self-dependence of enterprises and on the workers self-government groups' real participation in management. The necessary enactments should guarantee the fulfillment by the trade unions of the functions defined by Point One of this agreement.

Only a nation that is aware of its problems and that has a good knowledge of reality can sponsor and implement the program for streamlining the economy. The government will radically expand the range of the socioeconomic information available to the nation, the trade unions and economic and social organizations.

In addition, the Interfactory Committee demands: To create lasting prospects for developing peasant family farms, which are the foundation of Polish agriculture; to ensure an equal access of all sectors access to all the means of production, including land; and to create conditions for the rebirth of rural self-government groups.

With regard to Point Seven that states: "To pay from the Central Trade Union Council funds all the employees who are on strike wages for the strike period and for annual leave," it was decided:

Employees in the work forces on strike will receive for the period of strike an advance payment of forty percent of their remuneration, and after they have resumed work, they will receive up to 100 percent of the outstanding difference of their remuneration calculated as for a period of the annual leave based on the eight-hour day. The Interfactory Strike Committee appeals to the work forces associated within it that—after the strike has ended and in cooperation with the managements of factories, work enterprises and other institutions—they should take action to increase productivity, to economize on materials and energy and to enhance conscientiousness in every job.

With regard to Point Eight that states: "To increase the basic wages of each employee by Z2,000 a month in compensation for the present price hikes," it was decided:

Gradual increases in the wages of all employee groups, above all in the lowest wages groups, will be effected. The principle was agreed that wages will be increased in individual factories and in groups of branches. These increases are being implemented and will be implemented in keeping with the specifics of trade, professions and branches and will seek to upgrade remuneration by a single pay step or by suitably increasing other elements of remuneration or of the wage group. As for office workers in enterprises, their remuneration will be raised by a single pay step in their personal wages. These pay raises now under discussion will be completed by the end of September of this year in accordance with branch accords.

Having analyzed all branches, the government, in cooperation with the trade unions, will present by October 31 of this year a program for increasing, as of January 1, 1981, the wages of the lowest earners, giving special consideration to the families with many children.

With regard to Point Nine that states: "To guarantee an automatic increase in wages parallel to increase in prices and to the loss of the value of money," it was decided:

It is necessary to check the increases in the prices for staple goods by increasing the control over the socialized and the private sectors, in particular by stopping the so-called stealthy price hikes.

In keeping with the government's decision, research will be conducted into the development of living costs. This research will also be conducted by the trade unions and scientific institutes. By the end of 1980 the government will work out the principles of compensation for the increases in the cost of living. These principles will be subjected to a public discussion and, when agreed upon, will be implemented. They should take into account the issue of the social minimum (minimum subsistence level).

With regard to Point Ten that states: "To ensure complete supplies of food for the domestic market and to export only and exclusively surpluses" (of food) and to Point Eleven that states: "To abolish commercial prices and sales for hard currencies under the scheme of so-called internal export," and to Point Thirteen that states: "To introduce meat rationing—food coupons (until the market situation is mastered)," it was decided:

Meat supplies for the population will be improved by December 31 of this year by various measures including: increased profitability of farm production, restricting meat exports to a necessary minimum, and additional meat imports. Also within the same time a program will be presented for improving meat supplied to the population and for eventual meat rationing by way of coupons.

It was agreed that the Pewex shops (selling for hard currencies) will not sell the staple consumer goods produced in Poland that are in short supply. The nation will be informed by the end of the year about the decisions and measures concerning the supplies to the market.

The Interfactory Strike Committee has asked for the liquidation of the commercial shops and streamlining and standardizing meat prices at an average level.

With regard to Point Twelve that states: "To introduce the principles by which leading and managing cadres are selected by virtue of their qualifications and not party affiliation and to abolish the privileges of the citizens' militia, the security service and the party apparatus through equalizing the family allowances, liquidating special sales and so on" it was decided:

The demand is accepted that the leading and managing cadres should be consistently selected in keeping with the principle of qualifications and abilities of the members of the party, of the (other political) parties and of nonparty people. The program for equalizing the family allowances for all the trade groups will be presented by the government by December 31, 1980. The government commission states that only employees' restaurants and canteens like those in other work establishments and offices are operated [sentence as published, probably reference to militia ATC privileges].

With regard to Point Fourteen that states: "To lower the retirement age of women to 50 and of men to 55 or to 30 years worked in the Polish People's Republic by women and 35 years by men regardless of their ages," it was decided:

The government commission regards this demand as impossible to fulfill now in view of the country's present economic and demographic situation. The issue can be discussed in the future.

The Interfactory Strike Committee has asked to examine this issue by December 31, 1980 and to consider the possibility of allowing employees doing strenuous jobs to retire five years earlier (30 years for women and 35 years for men, and in the case of particularly strenuous jobs [to advance retirement age] by at least 15 years. [sentence as published] This should take place only at the request of the employee.

With regard to Point Fifteen that states: "To equalize the pensions and annuities of the so-called old scheme so that they are even with the present-scheme pensions and annuities," it was decided:

The government commission declares that increases in the lowest pensions and annuities will be effected annually, consistent with the country's economic potential, and will take into account the increases in the lowest wages. The government will present an implementation program by December 31, 1980. The government will propose that the lowest pensions and annuities be raised to the level of the so-called social minimum determined by the research carried out by the appropriate institutes, presented to the public and controlled by the trade unions. The Interfactory Strike Committee stresses the extreme urgency of this issue and maintains its demand that the pensions and annuities of the old and new scheme be at the same level and that increases in the costs of living be taken into account.

With regard to Point Sixteen that states: "To improve the working conditions of the health services so as to ensure complete medical care for the working persons," it was decided:

It is considered necessary to immediately increase the investment capacities of the health services, to improve the supply of medicines through additional imports of raw materials, to increase the wages of all health service workers (to change the wage scale for nurses) and to urgently draw up government and departmental programs for improving the state of the nation's health.

With regard to Point Seventeen that states: "To ensure the necessary vacancies in creches and kindergardens for working women's children," it was decided:

The government commission fully agrees with the importance of this demand. The voivodship authorities will present the necessary program by November 30, 1980.

With regard to Point Eighteen that states: "To grant maternity leave for three years in order to raise the baby," it was decided:

By December 31, 1980 an analysis will be carried out—in

cooperation with the trade unions—of the national economy's potential and the length of the leave and the amount of the monthly payment will be determined for women on maternity leave (now unpaid) to take care of their babies. The Interfactory Strike Committee demands that such an analysis consider a payment equivalent to the full wages in the first year after the baby was born and to 50 percent of these wages in the second year, but not lower than Z2,000 a month. This demand should be met gradually, beginning with the first half-year of 1981.

With regard to Point Nineteen that states: "To reduce the waiting period for apartments," it was decided:

By December 31, 1980 the voivodship authorities will present a program for improving the housing situation in order to reduce the waiting time for apartments. This program will be extensively discussed by the people of the voivodship and will be in consultation with the appropriate organizations (the Association of Polish Urbanists—TUP; the Association of the Architects of the Polish Republic—SARP; the Chief Technical Organization—NOT; and so on). The program also should consider the present utilization of the existing plants turning out housing components and the further development of the production base of construction trades. The same measures will be taken countrywide.

With regard to Point Twenty that states: "To increase travel allowances from Z40 to Z100 and to increase the family separation allowance," it was decided:

As of January 1, 1981 the size of travel allowances and the separation allowance will be increased. The proposals in this regard will be presented by the government by October 31, 1980.

With regard to Point Twenty-One that states: "To make all Saturdays workfree, and the employees working on shifts and under the four-brigade system to be compensated for Saturdays by an increased annual leave allowance or by other paid days off," it was decided:

We will work out and present by December 31, 1980 principles and methods of implementing the program for paid workfree Saturdays as well as other methods of regulating a shorter working time. This program will provide for a larger number of paid workfree Saturdays as early as 1981.

Having made the aforementioned decisions, the following agreement was reached:

The government pledges:

To ensure personal security and honor the present working conditions of the participants in the present strike and of the persons helping them; to examine at the ministerial level the specific problems of the branches as submitted by the workforces of all the striking factories associated with the Interfactory Strike Committee; to immediately publicize the full text of the protocol of this agreement in the national mass media (the press, radio and television).

The Interfactory Strike Commitee pledges to end the strike at 1700 hours on August 31, 1980.

[Signed] The presidium of the Interfactory Strike Committee:

Chairman Lech Walesa
Vice Chairman Andrzej Kolodziej
Vice Chairman Bogdan Lis

Members: Lech Badkowski, Wojciech Gruszewski, Andrzej Gwiazda, Stefan Izbedski; Jerzy Kwiecik, Zdzislaw Kobylinski, Henryka Krzywonos, Stefan Lewandowski, Alina Pienkowska, Jozef Przybylski, Jerzy Sikorski, Lech Lobieszek, Tadeusz Stanny, Anna Walentynowicz, and Florian Wisniewski.

The government commission:

Chairman Mieczyslaw Jagielski, vice chairman of the Council of Ministers of the Polish People's Republic.

Members: Zbigniew Zielinski, member of the PZPR Central Committee Secretariat; Tadeusz Fiszbach, chairman of the voivodship People's Council in Gdansk; Jerzy Kolodziejski, voivode of Gdansk.

Rumanian Documents

The SLOMR Charter

The following document, dated February 1979, is the Charter of the Free Trade Union of Rumanian workers, known by its Rumanian acronym SLOMR. Source: AFL-CIO Free Trade Union News, *May 1979.*

In Bucharest there was established in February 1979, in accordance with Article 22 of the International Covenant on Civil and Political Rights and in accordance with Article 8 of the Covenant on Economic, Social, and Cultural Rights, granted by Decree 212 of the Council of State of Rumania on October 1, 1974, the Free Trade Union of Rumanian Workers, SLOMR.

A list of the founding members of this union along with their individual employment is annexed to this text.

SLOMR declares itself affiliated with the International Confederation of Free Trade Unions. It declares itself in solidarity with the activity of every organization in Rumania and abroad that fights for the respect for the fundamental rights of man, and especially those rights that are derived through labor relationships.

The creation of SLOMR has become an objective necessary because of the economic, social, and cultural situations in Rumania. The formation of SLOMR is a perfectly legal act being constituted according to the laws of the country and according to the international agreements that Rumania has verified in Decree 212 of 1974. Likewise Articles 8 and 22, respectively, of the Economic, Social, and Cultural Rights, provide that every man has the right to associate himself freely with others, including the right to constitute a trade union and to adhere himself to it for the protection of his own interests. These trade unions have the right to function freely and to affiliate themselves with international trade union organizations. SLOMR does not propose any actions of a political character (it distinguishes between the defense of the political rights of citizens and actions of a purely political nature). Hence it is clear in the name SLOMR that it exercises its activities freely and is not a conveyor of any political force, and it takes this lead from the valuable, official affirmations of 1971, which state, "From here on trade unions will not be conveyors of political ideologies." This is a precious indication that unfortunately has been strangely forgotten along with many other such indications. SLOMR proposes to fight for the defense of the rights of Rumanian citizens, in virtue of the Universal Declaration of the Rights of Man, ratified by Rumania in the aforementioned decree. The declaration proclaims the ideal of the human being freed from fear, and SLOMR militates for putting into effect Article 11 of the Covenent on Economic, Social, and Cultural Rights that provides the right of every man to a sufficient standard of living, with respect to food, clothing, and habitation.

SLOMR begins from the premise that these elementary rights must be realized here in Rumania without discrimination and that the hope for realization of these natural desires of the human being do not lie in one's fleeing his own country. SLOMR, however, does emphatically support Article 212 of the Covenant on Civil and Political Rights (ratified by Decree 212) which declares that "every man is free to leave any country (including his own) and is free to return to his own country."

SLOMR proposes especially to fight for the respect for the rights of Rumanian citizens, with respect to labor relationships. Hence it accepts the numerous restructurings that have resulted in the reduction of personnel from various factories and institutions which have taken place in recent years as a result of the economic difficulties confronting the country. These difficulties derive from the desire to bring Rumania in a short time to a high standard of living. This is a desire we all share. There are, nevertheless, many Rumanian citizens unable to find work at this time.

Unfortunately, official statistics do not show at all the true situation of unemployment in our country. The Law of Pensions passed in the summer of 1977 stirred up a wave of dissidence resulting in a strike (of the coalminers of the Jiu Valley) and created the undesirable situation in which many elderly people still able to work could not find employment in conditions similar to the relatively advantageous conditions found under the former law regarding pensions. There are numerous cases of forced retirements of elderly people for so-called psychiatric reasons. These are usually people who for a long time were felt to be incompatible with the superstructure of the regime due to their convictions. Those who have suffered prolonged imprisonment for their convictions have not had their years of detention recognized as time spent in employment (a right granted to prisoners up until 1944). Such people receive a pension for sickness or retirement that is unable to assure them of sufficient food, clothing, and habitation. Some receive no pension at all, not having the necessary time or seniority, thus violating the aforementioned Decree 212.

The presently employed are subjected to supplementary burdens of work that far exceed their capacity for work. This is due to the reduction of personnel in the factories which is combined with the increased goals and demands for promotion. This situation leads to sickness, absenteeism, and the falling off of production. Under such conditions there is no place for a corresponding increase in wages, and the wages that exist are totally inadequate.

SLOMR pronounces firmly that the activity of working men should take place in conditions that respect the rights of men; i.e., in an environment that is pleasant, that is heated, that is adequately lighted, in an area where health hazards are reduced, where free protection equipment is provided, and where free nourishment is provided. The providing of these things would transform the place of work from one of drudgery to one of pleasure and would result in increased output.

SLOMR proposes that the mobilization of citizens for so-called political work should be carried out not by coercion but on a voluntary basis, as it is well known that the Rumanian people have always been hardworking and ready to go far beyond the call of duty. The eventual absenteeism of a person or group of people should not be followed by persecution. SLOMR proposes that the mobilization of workers for rallies and other demonstrations should be on a voluntary basis within decent limits; i.e., without disturbing the activities of the factory and without coercion.

SLOMR militates for the respect of the right to a weekly rest and calls for an increase in free time for those employed. SLOMR does not encourage slothfulness, careerism, or opportunism, which are singled out by the official press as isolated cases and not as the current symptomatic norm of Rumanian society.

SLOMR proposes the integration of the special party stores and other units of closed-circuit distribution of goods to party members into the general society. This would lead to a diversification of consumer goods and a more adequate nourishment of the citizens.

SLOMR proposes that the special hotels and houses for members of the party be converted into hospitals, old-folks homes, clinics, or hotels open to the public.

Likewise we propose the reduction to decent limits of the modes of car transportation offered to the organs of the superstructure, and we invite these people to use as much as possible the modes of transportation commonly used by the general citizenry. This would lead to real savings of fuel and energy so needed for the development of our heavy industry.

SLOMR proposes an efficient control of the financial activities of organs of the superstructure.

SLOMR strives to bring to public awareness, both here and abroad, cases of non-respect for human rights in Rumania, mentioned above in conformity with Article 19 of the International Convenant on Civil and Political Rights and ratified by Decree 212 of the Council of States. This article says that "every person is free to gather and to spread ideas of any kind across any border by any printed or written means."

In this sense, SLOMR makes an appeal to every citizen deprived of his rights to alert us to their particular situation, especially with regard to labor rights, by contacting in writing:

Dr. Ionel Cana
Box 17 Julesti
Post Restant
Bucharest 7700

and by calling him on the telephone at 50-71-62 to inform him that a letter has been sent. Such contacts will be considered as acts of membership in the SLOMR. We appeal to our potential adherents to address themselves to us without fear, taking into consideration that they are addressing fellow citizens and not officers of a hegemonistic power, for SLOMR is a free association of citizens constituted in respect of Decree 212 of the Council of State.

SLOMR makes an appeal to the government of Rumania with regard to the censorship of mail: respect the provisions of Article 17 of the Covenant on Civil and Political Rights ratified by Decree 212, which underline the inviolability of correspondence. Even if they do control the contents of letters, we ask that they allow them to reach their destination.

SLOMR, being in essence an organizatoin for the dispensation of human rights and being without a budget initially, provides that adherence to it does not necessarily presuppose any subscription.

SLOMR makes an appeal to the superstructure of Rumania that by open dialogue they might contribute to the favorable solution of the cases brought up. Recognition by Rumania, before its own people and before international public opinion, that cases of violation of human rights do exist in Rumania would be a point of pride for Rumania before all the people of the civilized world. It would contribute to the international prestige of Rumania and would be an asset to the international economic support so needed for the Great Program of Multilateral Development being carried out by Rumania. If the United States of America, a country which has already arrived at the highest level of standard of living and of civilization, is not afraid to alert international public opinion to its own cases of non-respect for human rights, how much more prestigious and praiseworthy would this act be for Rumania.

There exists the possibility that we, the founders of SLOMR will be crushed and physically and morally broken by the perfectionist apparatus of repression. Any denouncement by any one of us of the principles here pronounced, we declare null and void, as it would have been obtained by force or repression. We can be annihilated, but the ideals for which we fight will not perish as long as there is a Rumanian in his land. We are sure that others, younger and more courageous than us, will come and will lead further the inextinguishable flame of dignity of man in Rumania.

The Free Trade Union of Rumanian Workers
Bucharest, Rumania
February 1979

The following are the founding members of SLOMR:
From Bucharest:
Dr. Ionel Cana, physician, general practitioner
Gheorghe Brasoveanu, economist
Nicolae Gugu, veteran member of the Communist Party, former volunteer in the Spanish Civil War
Gheorghe Fratila, cameraman

From the city of Turnu-Severin:
Ioana Grigore, C.P. employee
Ilie Blidaru, welder
Costel Haritoian, tinsmith

Endre Molnar, tinsmith
Romulus Bondea, riveter
Nicolae Mutu, foundry-worker
Aurelian Paunescu, foundry-worker
Vasile Otel, fitter
Aurel Mustachide, riveter
Nicolae Balamat, welder
Elena Pasmagius, welder
Victoria Ivanovici, electrician
Frosa Pesteanu, charwoman
Mihai Gheorghiu, electrician
Petre Papa, welder
Romica Badiu, welder

Over 2,500 Support Free Trade Union

The following SLOMR communique was issued on March 6, 1979. Source: Labor Focus on Eastern Europe.

Following the publication of the SLOMR Founding Declaration on March 4, 1979, the milling-machine operator Virgil Chender, representing the Unofficial Trade Union of Workers, Peasants, and Soldiers of Mures County, came to see Dr. Ionel Cana, the initiator of SLOMR. The Mures union was set up clandestinely at the end of 1978, and according to its representative, had no less than 1,487 members. They do not have a list of names: the trade unionists know one another by numbers going up to 1,487.

Dr. Ionel Cana argued that a trade union association ought not to be a conspiratorial grouping and that a trade union does not pursue political aims. The laws and international agreements signed by Rumania—especially State Council Decree 212 of 1974—allow for trade unions to engage in free activity and to affiliate with other trade union organizations, including international bodies, with the aim of protecting the interests of working people. And so, he maintained, it is not justified for such a numerous trade union organization to be clandestine.

Virgil Chender expressed his agreement with these views concerning the openness of the Unofficial Trade Union of the Workers, Peasants, and Soldiers of Mures County. Moreover, considering the striking similarity between the 24 points of the Mures union's program and the statement of aims in the SLOMR Founding Declaration, he proposed that the Mures union should be incorporated into SLOMR with the addition of a few necessary points to its statement of aims.

We shall mention these additions after we have listed some of the 1,487 Mures unionists. The list was reconstituted from memory by their representative. The other members should affiliate with SLOMR by means of signed letters addressed to: Dr. Ionel Cana, Bucuresti, Oficiul Postal 47, Giulesti, Post Restant, Cod 7700. They should also contact us by telephone at one of the following Bucharest numbers: 17-59-46; 88-65-40; 50-71-62, communicating their name, address, and telephone number if they have one.

Here is the first list of SLOMR members from Sighisoara:
Virgil Chender, Str. Vasile, Lucaci, 12, Sighisoara, Judetz Mures
Ioan Coman, Str. Closca, 47, Sighisoara, Judetz Mures
Aurel Militoriu, Str. Cinepii, 35, Sighisoara, Judetz Mures
Dietmar Wolff, Str. Gh. Gh. Dej, 93, Sighisoara, Judetz Mures
Edmond Gabor, Str. Florilor, Bloc I, Sighisoara, Judetz Mures
Carol Fulop, Str. Ilarie Chendi, 83, Sighisoara, Judetz Mures
Alexandra Bran, Str. Primaverii, 20a, Sighisoara, Judetz Mures
Imre Lukacs, Str. Ana Ipatescu, 20, Sighisoara, Judetz Mures
Elena Stef, Str. Pastorilor, 17, Sighisoara, Judetz Mures

And now we shall quote a few lines from the introduction to the 24 points mentioned above, adding two facsimiles from these documents in order to prove their authenticity:

> We who are many throughout the country are suffering, live badly and in need, while the few live well, have everything, go in want of nothing. We have nobody to turn to, no one listens to us, no one understands or wants to know anything about us. We are always promised, from one five-year plan to the next, that we shall live better; but in fact we live worse and worse.

Of the 24 points, we shall also quote those which are being added to the SLOMR statement of aims:

> The worker must be free to move from one factory to another and from one agricultural cooperative to another, wherever he thinks he can live better.

> Members of cooperatives must be free to sell their own products on

the market and must no longer be contracted on disadvantageous terms to sell lambs, calves, pigs, wool, and other products.

The pensions of cooperative workers must be the same as those given to factory workers, since a pension of 150 lei is enough only for a few days.

People doing their national service should no longer be forced to put their tongues out during instruction, to go into cold water during the winter, or to stay wet for hours on end. As things are, the soldier lives the life of a convict.

The Rumanian government must abolish terror, beating, imprisonment, and internment of those fighting for human rights. This is a barbaric practice, unworthy of the times in which we are living.

We should all be brothers, creators of a dignified, free, and happy life on our planet—the planet of human beings, not of beasts in the forest.

The SLOMR is very happy to adopt these principles, written in the forceful style of the working people.

SLOMR also announces the membership of English-language teacher Nicolae Dascalu, Str. Valea Ialomitei, 1a, Bloc C18A, Ap. 60, Sector 7, Bucharest. He was also a signatory of Mr. Paul Goma's appeal to the Belgrade Conference. Other new members include: Ilie Dascalu, the younger brother of Nicolae; and Ion Marandici, a teacher of mathematics living at Str. Valea Argesului, 9, Bloc 17, Scara A, Et. 4, Ap. 13, Bucharest. He has been told of other educational workers in Rumania who are about to join SLOMR.

SLOMR
Bucharest
March 6, 1979

Police Drive Against SLOMR

The following information about repressive measures against SLOMR was communicated in April 1979 by phone to Rumanian exiles in Paris who taperecorded it.

1. We demand that opinion polls be conducted, with the participation of the world trade union movement, in the factories, educational, cultural, and other institutions, as well as in the villages, concerning the need for SLOMR to exist. We demand that our program be made known through the Rumanian press, radio, and television, and that we be able to rent an office and enjoy the same rights as the state-run union.

2. We wish to communicate the following protest: We vehemently protest against the brutal methods employed against SLOMR members. We protest against the methods of intimidation used by the Securitate in relation to those who wish to join SLOMR. We vehemently protest against the abuse of state laws and decrees in order to hit at citizens demanding their rights. We demand the immediate release of the founder-members of SLOMR. We demand an immediate end to beatings-up, to the disconnections of telephones, to the interception of correspondence, to arrests at people's homes, to street-kidnapping, to the war of nerves with all its terrorist methods of intimidation. We demand the release of all those tried and imprisoned not for committing crimes but for demanding their rights. We call for the support of all honest and worthy citizens of Rumania, on whom depends the existence of the whole state, including the existence of the people who are seeking to suppress our legal rights. We ask the international trade union movement and all human rights organizations to support our protest to the Rumanian government.

This protest is also the first action of the Bucharest Amnesty International group, set up on March 6, 1979.

3. Every SLOMR member is entitled to admit new members, and every request for membership should be duly signed by the new member.

4. Other points:

It is very important that the SLOMR program be read out again [on Radio Free Europe], since many people were not able to hear it before, at least in its entirety.

On Saturday, March 31, Colonel Miu of the "counter-information" service of the Bucharest Securitate, accompanied by a huge, giant-like policeman, forcibly entered the apartment of Professor Dascalu when he was not at home. They shouted at the professor's wife, who was holding their four-month-old daughter in her arms, and threatened their friends, Rodica and Bogdan Meschiu, who were then paying a visit. The policemen stayed for more than two hours and issued a series of threats, in particular the threat of "years and years in jail." Before leaving, they asked that the professor should present himself to the Securitate on Monday, April 2, or Tuesday, April 3. (This same Miu, in charge of interrogating Dascalu, had previously insulted, beaten and terrorized him, and threatened him with death, having kidnapped him off the street.) On April 3, Securitate agents returned to the professor's home, asked if he was back in Bucharest, and renewed their "invitation." We mention this case because it is a good example of the war of nerves launched by the Securitate against SLOMR members.

At the same time, a frenzied campaign has been unleashed to discredit SLOMR members. All kinds of rumors are spread: "They are all mad; paranoids." "Dr. Cana had a brain operation," "the economist Brasoveanu is a paranoid," and so on. No less use is found for diversion: those who have applied for passports are promised that all their problems will be solved so long as they give up their activities.

We do not know what Dr. Cana is charged with. The Securitate has arranged for various official channels to let it be known that he is under arrest. Often in an ironic way: "Oh, can't you find him? All you have to do is look." In other words, he has disappeared. There is no charge.

We would like a world trade union body or a national union to get in touch with us, to ask us for the information we have.

We are organizing in Bucharest a committee that will remain in existence until Dr. Cana and the others are released. We shall send you details as they become available.

Czechoslovakia Documents

Charter Document No. 7 on Social and Economic Rights

Charter 77, a broad-based human rights movement, was founded in early 1977 following the Czechoslovak government's ratification of the International Covenant on Civil and Political Rights and the International Covenant on Economic, Social, and Cultural Rights on March 23, 1976 and their publication in the official media on November 11, 1976. Source: Labour Focus on Eastern Europe.

Both pacts on which the Charter is based are imbued with the democratic ideal of the free human being. We think it just to emphasize in this regard that the ideal of the liberation of man from fear and want had and has its most radical defender in the international workers' movement, which has formulated these rights in their most developed form. The socialist movement has placed, and continues to place, as its aim to create the conditions in which workers will not have to sell their labor power. One cannot, however, on account of this aim of the complete liberation of work, set aside the simple and immediate demand that the man who enters the labor market should be able to sell his labor power under the most favorable conditions; that he should not only have the right to work in the narrow sense of the word but also free choice; that he should receive for his work a wage guaranteeing a decent standard of living for his family; that he should have the right to organize in the factories or in other workplaces struggles for wages and other demands; that he should have the right to form free trade unions with the possibility of free activity, etc.

All these demands are now enacted in law in the international pact about economic, social, and cultural rights—see the Digest of the Laws of the C.S.R. No. 120/76, which has now become a part of the Czechoslovak legal code.

We, the signatories of Charter 77, citizens of different political opinions, express agreement with the provisions of this pact. On the basis of our deliberations, we have arrived at the conclusion that the state of economic and social rights in Czechoslovakia demands an unbiased evaluation, which we want to stimulate with this document.

One of the most important articles in the pact speaks about the right to work at a job which is "freely chosen or accepted" (Article 6). We often meet with statements to the effect that this right has already been realized in Czechoslovakia, and that as distinct from capitalism, there exists no unemployment here. It is true that the Czechoslovak workers have created the economic conditions which have abolished overt unemployment; the workers have in this respect more social security than in the other developed countries. This, however, has been achieved at a price which was not necessary for the abolition of unemployment. And it has produced a decline in economic efficiency and created widespread hidden unemployment, shown in the great number of superfluous institutions and working positions which could, by applying modern technology and organization of work, have long ago been done away with.

This state of affairs is accompanied by the de facto duty to be employed; the restriction on the right to choose, give up, or change one's place of work; and legal handicaps on the citizen who does not fulfill the increasingly strict demands of the state. The state is more or less the monopoly employer; the association of workers in cooperatives is ever more restricted; the cooperatives themselves are being brought increasingly under the control of the state organs. The possibility of a free choice of work is an inseparable component of the right to work; in fact, normal practice and the labor code go only a little way toward meeting this aspect of the right to work. In recent years there has even been a tendency for the labor laws and practice to get worse in this respect....

Both the practice of the trade union movement and the legal norms concerning association in unions are at variance with the right of union organizations to "free activity" (Article 8), for they do not admit the "right to found union organizations" or the "right to join the union organization of one's own choice" (Article 8). In the unions, it is not the blue- and white-collar workers but economic and other apparatuses which make the decisions. The function which the unions played for long decades in defending the basic interests of the workers has practically disappeared. It has been forgotten for a long time now that in the first years after World War II there existed, alongside the unions and independent workers' organs, factory councils with extensive powers including management functions and with an impressive activity in the political and socioeconomic fields; it is also forgotten that the post-May 1945 workers' councils found their continuation in the workers' councils of 1968.

The attitude of workers to their work at that time is revealed in a sociological investigation carried out in 1969:

Interest in work	**Until August 1968**	**After August 1968**
much more	46.8%	0.9%
somewhat more	20.1%	2.6%
no change	21.0%	11.3%
somewhat less	4.9%	14.2%
much less	3.1%	68.1%
can't decide	4.2%	2.8%

The unions do not ensure that broad layers of the workers take part in formulating wage policy either at the local or the overall level. They allow this policy to be decided from above; when the workers resist the lowering of wages, as for example during the rationalization of the wage system in 1973-75, the unions do not stand by their side. If the workers go on strike—at the risk of persecution, which is in conflict with the right to strike, so that it doesn't often happen—the unions betray them. Nor do the unions try to make the government work out the minimum necessary for existence, which could be adjusted each year, and which could form the basis for determining the minimum wage.

The union organizations have at their disposal all kinds of information about the state of security of work and about the living conditions of the workers; they have at their disposal data about the real lowering of wages by hidden and overt inflation, and they are often made aware of the mess in the management of accommodation. In none of these directions, however, do they bring pressure to bear for basic solutions. Instead of launching a struggle for participation in basic economic decision-making, they abandon the field and thus bear a common responsibility for bureaucratic decision-making.

The unions take part in moralizing campaigns about the full use of working time, but the real opinions and interests of the workers in this question are not expressed. It is true, and everyone knows it, that Czechoslovakia has perhaps the shortest working time in the world; much less than the established working time is *actually* worked, often in tacit agreement with the management. But everyone also knows that if one considers overtime and Saturday and Sunday mornings, the Czechoslovak workers have one of the longest working weeks, at least in Europe. This paradox is not accidental. It is the consequence of unrestrained attempts by the workers to achieve just payment by the ways which, in the given situation—under conditions of a generally low standard of living and organization of work—appear the most obvious. For this reason, the worker husbands his labor power and does not achieve the efficiency which could be achieved. The "saved" labor power is then used in overtime or is sold on the black market. In this sphere in fact there is a strong stimulus from the high demand for services of various kinds. The remuneration for overtime is in fact an important part of the wage for most workers.

The trade union organization does not take any productive standpoint toward this complex problem of the national economy, although a whole gamut of possibilities offer themselves, like the participation of all union members in judging the real length of working time, the possibility of its shortening, at least to the legal time of 42½ hours, while maintaining the present level of wages or even raising it in some sectors.

But to expect the unions, which have become appendages of the economic apparatus, to take up the right of workers for a just remuneration and for the development of a radical initiative in this direction would be wholly unrealistic. This fact, however, should not become a handy alibi for anyone who has anything to do with these matters. For each "individual, having a duty toward others and toward the society to which he belongs, is in duty bound to strengthen and uphold the rights recognized in this pact [preamble to the pact about economic, social, and cultural rights]."

In connection with many questions, we could take note of many positive developments, especially in comparison with the past. The essential thing, however, lies not in adding up the pluses and minuses in the field of social and economic rights, but in what attitude one takes to them. We consider it to be the duty of every citizen to express disagreement with the notion that the worker has full social rights and that these rights are all assured, and especially with the idea that the realization of the right to work and certain other basic social rights deprives all the remaining rights—above all, the political and democratic rights—of their significance.

It is true that the workers no longer sell their labor power in a capitalist market of the old type. But this does not mean that all their rights are automatically respected. Only the working people themselves can guarantee their interests and rights. If their role in this is restricted, curtailed, or even prevented, so that they are denied civil and political rights, this has an inevitably negative effect throughout the whole of socioeconomic life. In agreement with the pact about social and economic rights, we are convinced that "the ideal of the free human being, free from fear and want, can only be achieved if the conditions are created in which each will be able to enjoy economic, social, and cultural rights, alongside their civil and political rights [preamble to the pact]."

With similar urgency we would like to remind people that the aim and meaning of socialism is not only the simple assurance of social rights and security, but also the all-sided development of man as a free being—the liberation of humanity in the deepest and most meaningful sense of those words. There is still much to be done to achieve this aim. This would apply even in a situation where we in Czechoslovakia enjoyed social and economic rights not only on a much higher level than today, but even to the extent which is guaranteed to us by the international pact on economic, social, and cultural rights.

Professor Jan Patocka
Professor Jiri Hajek
Prague
March 8, 1977

About the Authors

Adrian Karatnycky has written on Soviet and East European affairs for *The New Republic, Commonweal, The New Leader, National Review, Inquiry,* and other journals. He has served as chairman of the Committee for the Defense of Soviet Political Prisoners and as assistant director of the International Sakharov Hearings. He is currently research director of the A. Philip Randolph Institute.

Alexander J. Motyl is the author of *The Turn to the Right: The Ideological Origins and Development of Ukrainian Nationalism, 1919-1929* and of numerous articles on the Soviet Union and Eastern Europe. Born in 1953 and a resident of New York City, he is currently pursuing his doctoral studies in Soviet affairs.

Adolph Sturmthal is the author of *The Tragedy of European Labor, 1918-1939* and of numerous books and articles on the international labor movement. Born in Vienna, he was editor of several European journals until coming to the United States in 1938. He has taught at a number of American universities, including Columbia, Yale, and Cornell, and has lectured on labor subjects in Japan, Singapore, Canada, France, and Malaysia. He has also served as consultant to a number of government agencies and to business and labor organizations. He is currently emeritus professor of labor and industrial relations at the University of Illinois, Urbana-Champaign.

League for Industrial Democracy

The League for Industrial Democracy was established in 1905 by Upton Sinclair, Clarence Darrow, Jack London, and other social visionaries of the time. It is a publicly supported non-profit, tax-exempt membership organization which conducts research and educational programs with a special focus on trade unionism, social policy, and human rights.